D1379248

GAZA

Daily work goes on. It goes into the ground, into crops, into children's bellies and their bright eyes. Good things don't get lost... the very least you can do in your life is figure out what you hope for. And the most you can do is live inside that hope.

Barbara Kingsolver, *Animal Dreams*, Scribner's, 1991

GAZA

BENEATH THE BOMBS

Sharyn Lock with Sarah Irving

Afterword by Richard Falk

PlutoPress
www.plutobooks.com

For Eva, *ma felfel*. For Vik, to put with the broken *shisha* glass.
For my Gaza sisters and brothers, and for each irreplaceable child.

First published 2010 by Pluto Press
345 Archway Road, London N6 5AA and
175 Fifth Avenue, New York, NY 10010

www.plutobooks.com

Distributed in the United States of America exclusively by
Palgrave Macmillan, a division of St. Martin's Press LLC,
175 Fifth Avenue, New York, NY 10010

British Library Cataloguing in Publication Data
A catalogue record for this book is available from the British Library

ISBN   978 0 7453 3025 9   Hardback
ISBN   978 0 7453 3024 2   Paperback

Library of Congress Cataloging in Publication Data applied for

This book is printed on paper suitable for recycling and made from fully managed
and sustained forest sources. Logging, pulping and manufacturing processes are
expected to conform to the environmental standards of the country of origin.

10   9   8   7   6   5   4   3   2   1

Designed and produced for Pluto Press by
Chase Publishing Services Ltd, 33 Livonia Road, Sidmouth, EX10 9JB, England
Typeset from disk by Stanford DTP Services, Northampton, England
Printed and bound in the European Union by
CPI Antony Rowe, Chippenham and Eastbourne

CONTENTS

ACKNOWLEDGEMENTS

Sarah, whose idea this book was, who gave me confidence and did all the hard bits. Everyone at Pluto Press, particularly David, who took me through the publication process remarkably painlessly. My fellow Free Gaza founders and all those who've been working on sending boats ever since I jumped ship. Your humour and determination kept me going, and you made my dream of returning to Palestine come true. My ISM gang, with whom I was proud to work despite us all driving each other crazy. Our West Bank support team, who gave us every bit of support they could think of. Gaza cafes Delice, Marna House, and Mazaj, whose staff seemed happy to consider one cup of tea purchased every three hours as a fair exchange for Eva's and my daily use of their internet facilities. My favourite Faraheen, Jabalia, and Zaytoun families. We love you.

The Gaza medics and hospital staff, with whom it was an honour and privilege to spend time. Your courage, steadfastness and humour in the face of danger leave me without words. *Ya'tiikum il-Afiya wa elf, elf shukran lekum.* My brilliant friends in my various homes and countries, who kept me going with donations and supportive international phone calls. I cannot overstate what generosity this represented when something like buying juice is normally a luxury for most of us! My father, who watched documentaries with me and encouraged me to think logically. My mother, who taught me the importance of compassion above all things, and passed on her own mother's adage: 'If you see something that needs doing, then do it yourself.' (And then they were surprised when I became an activist…) And the two people whose lives I make most difficult, but who, for mysterious reasons of their own, seem willing to continue loving me anyway. One gets to do it from a distance; the other has to do it in person – almost every day.

In the text, some names have been changed to protect privacy.

We have done our best to check all our facts, but while I was writing from Gaza I was aware that language issues and the chaos of war could lead to errors. Any such remaining are entirely my responsibility.

INTRODUCTION

Sarah Irving

In summer 2001, with the Second Intifada less than a year old, Palestinians, Israelis and internationals confronted increasing Israeli repression in the West Bank by forming the International Solidarity Movement. 'ISM', according to its website, 'aims to support and strengthen the Palestinian popular resistance by providing the Palestinian people with two resources, international protection and a voice with which to nonviolently resist an overwhelming military occupation force.'[1]

From Israeli women in Salfit using the tactics of Western environmentalists to try and stop settlers destroying olive trees, to American students in urban areas living as 'human shields' in family homes during military incursions, a group started to coalesce. Over Christmas 2001 around 80 people – mainly European and American – answered a call to spend two weeks travelling round the West Bank and Gaza, digging up roadblocks, bearing witness as Palestinians carried out peaceful demonstrations and meeting political and community leaders. They even managed to flypost an Israeli tank outside Nablus with the martyr posters of a man killed standing on his balcony a few days before.

A similar call for support went out for Easter 2002, but plans to move around the West Bank in a similar way took a radically different turn when the Israeli military launched Operation Defensive Shield, a major re-occupation of all Palestinian towns and cities in the West Bank and Gaza. Some ISMers ended up as human shields with Yasser Arafat in his Ramallah compound, others in the Church of the Nativity or in refugee camps in Nablus and Bethlehem, or with Palestine Indymedia. This set the scene for long-term ISM tactics of providing witnesses and accompaniment for Palestinians engaging in non-violent resistance, such as the demonstrations against the Separation Wall at villages like Budrus, Biddu, Ni'lin and Bi'lin.

With its first deliberate attacks on international activists in 2002, Israel upped the ante in a way that culminated in the killings in 2003 of Rachel Corrie and Tom Hurndall in Gaza. But finding that even crushing them to death with Caterpillar bulldozers or shooting them dead did not deter ISM activists, Israel developed the Blacklist. From the start of ISM some activists had been denied entry to Israel and therefore to Palestine, all of whose borders are controlled by Israel, but after 2003 this means of keeping international witnesses from viewing Israel's human rights abuses became more systematic. More and more individuals found that gaining accreditation for peace conferences or even changing their names by deed poll wouldn't gain them passage into Palestine.

In 2006, a small group of these blacklisted individuals – including Sharyn Lock – decided that if the land borders into the West Bank were closed to them, they would attempt to break the Israeli blockade of Gaza by sea. Israel's 2005 claim that it had washed its hands of Gaza gave weight to the claim that, since the blacklisted activists were not passing through Israeli territory, the Israeli authorities had no right or need to stop them.

Despite threats and at times physical aggression from Israeli naval vessels, several Free Gaza boats did indeed succeed in taking human rights observers, journalists, medics and parliamentarians to Gaza in the autumn of 2008. They also brought out both international visitors and Gazans needing to leave, including students with visas for courses abroad who had been denied exit through the brutal vagaries of the Rafah crossing, and Palestinians who had simply been cut off from overseas family for too long to bear.

But with the Israeli military's Operation Cast Lead offensive, launched in the closing days of 2008, Free Gaza's boats were blocked by the navy. A small number of international activists had foreseen this escalation after tensions started to rise with the end of a long-term quasi-ceasefire between Hamas and Israel.

Among them was Sharyn Lock, who had been an activist with ISM since 2002 and who also had some basic medic training. She therefore decided to stay in Gaza, not only as an international witness but also assisting the emergency services during the darkest days of the Israeli invasion. But she also managed to find time to report her experiences in the TalesToTell blog, which attracted thousands of readers across the world. One of those readers was myself who had been an ISM activist in the West Bank in 2001 and 2002. I worked with Sharyn to shape her daily tales of the horror of the Israeli invasion, the mundane brutalities of the siege and the tenderness, courage and humour of everyday Gazans into the book you are now holding.

During the 1948 *Nakba* – the 'Catastrophe' of the Palestinians when over 700,000 people fled their homes – over 200,000 refugees found their way to the tiny strip of land on the shores of the Mediterranean which is called Gaza (which previously had a population of only 60–80,000). For 20 years it remained under Egyptian control, until the Six Day War of 1967 when, along with the West Bank, it was occupied by Israel.

Gaza is almost entirely Sunni Muslim, with a small Christian community. Over 75% of its people are UNRWA-registered refugees (see p. 71), most of them living in eight camps or the neighbourhoods around them. But the poverty and desperation of besieged Gaza hides a long and rich history. Prehistoric humans passed through Gaza on their earliest journeys out of Africa, and ancient civilisations such as the Egyptians, Philistines and Assyrians established cities there. A key point on trade routes, it was home to marketplaces for spices, silks, wine, gold and olive oil. Vasco de Gama's discovery of a sea route to India heralded the decline of Gaza's international position, but under the Ottomans it became an important agricultural area, growing grains and later citrus. International influences also brought Gaza important creative traditions, including pottery, textiles, and an adventurous, spicy cuisine.[2]

The decades under Israeli rule have seen varying levels of conflict between occupier and occupied. With its massive refugee population – now around 1 million out of 1.4 million people – Gaza became known for the strength of its resistance, although large parts of its population were also dependent on jobs in Israel for their livelihoods.

The shooting of a truckload of Israel-bound Gazan labourers in 1987 was the spark which ignited the First Intifada,[3] the popular uprising which lasted until the deeply flawed 1993 Oslo Accords which brought the Palestine Liberation Organisation, which was founded in 1964, back to Palestine, in theory to begin the job of building a Palestinian state. With the beginning of the Intifada also came the birth of Hamas, the Islamist militant movement which helped to make religion a major factor in the until-then largely secular Palestinian resistance, and which became famous for sending suicide bombers – many of them from Gaza – into Israel.[4]

With its inadequate water supplies and cramped population, Gaza had few of the attractions of the West Bank for the Israeli state and, in a PR masterstroke, in 2005 Israel withdrew its settlements from Gaza. This allowed it to present itself to an uncritical Western media and ill-informed Western politicians as making a magnanimous gesture, restoring Gaza to its Palestinian population, whilst actually relieving itself of a large security bill and of the dissatisfaction of the many Israelis who resented expending cash and soldiers' lives defending a small number of largely religious extremist settlers. It also allowed Israel to cut off the fierce Gazan resistance behind a continuous closed border, while it carried on controlling access in and out of Israel via Erez and several other crossing points, and effectively governing movement in and out of Egypt through the Rafah crossing.

Disillusionment with Palestinian Authority corruption and the lack of progress in the development of a Palestinian state helped Hamas, to its own surprise as much as anyone else's, to win the Palestinian Legislative Council elections of January 2006.[5] Hamas formed a new government under Ismail Haniya, but Fatah (which still held the presidency) refused to relinquish power, so Hamas never managed to take control in the West Bank. The 'Quartet' – the USA, EU, UN and Russia – threatened to cut funds to Palestine on the grounds that Hamas was a terrorist organisation and Hamas-controlled Gaza was subjected by Israel to what was in effect an internationally-sanctioned siege. Always sporadic, Israeli permission to import basic goods – food, medical supplies, building materials – dried up almost entirely, and Israel started to withhold millions of dollars in tax revenue which should have been used to pay Palestinian public employees.[6]

The impacts of the siege on Gaza have been devastating. Food and fuel prices have spiralled, restricting people's diets and resulting in widespread malnutrition and vitamin deficiencies amongst children. 70% of the territory's population was estimated to be living in a state of food insecurity by late 2008[7] and 80% of the population was dependent on food aid due to high prices and massive unemployment.[8] The World Health

Organisation stated that 'Many hospitals were not fully functional before the current violence [Operation Cast Lead] due to shortages of drugs, medical supplies, spare parts, electricity and fuel',[9] and projects to improve Gaza's inadequate water and sanitation systems were halted due to lack of funds and building materials – leading in one case to the deaths of several people in a village flooded when the wall of a sewage reservoir collapsed.[10]

Trapped behind a largely impenetrable wall, Hamas and other Palestinian militant groups developed the tactic of firing rockets into Israeli towns on the other side of the border, most notably Sderot, although some Grad rockets with a range of up to 20km reached as far as Ashkelon. '3,278 rockets and mortar shells landed in Israeli territory [in 2008]. These numbers are double those of 2007 and 2006, years which marked a five-fold increase over prior years.' In early 2009, small numbers of a new type of rocket with a range of up to 40km reached Beersheba and Ashdod.[11] Some Palestinians and their supporters cited Israeli infringements of the ceasefire agreement with Hamas, Israel's refusal of Hamas's offer to extend the ceasefire period to a decade, and the disproportionate reporting of a few Israeli casualties compared to much larger numbers of Palestinian victims of Israeli armed operations. But with US and other political leaders providing emotive rhetoric about the misery of the people of Sderot, living under a 'hail' of rockets, the Israel government's PR machine presented the rockets as the perfect excuse to launch the massive Operation Cast Lead offensive on Gaza.

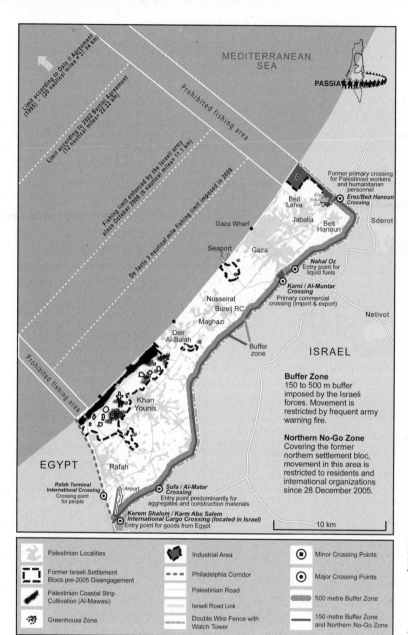

MEDITERRANEAN
SEA

PASSIA

Limit according to Oslo II Agreement
(1993) - (20 nautical miles = 37.04 km)

Limit according to 2002 Bertini Agreement
(12 nautical miles= 22.22 km)

Prohibited fishing area

Fishing limit enforced by the Israeli army
since October 2006 (6 nautical miles= 11.1 km)

De facto 3 nautical mile fishing limit imposed in 2008

Prohibited fishing area

Former primary crossing
for Palestinian workers
and humanitarian
personnel
*Erez/Beit Hanoun
Crossing*

Beit
Lahia

Erez
Industrial
Zone

Sderot

Jabalia

Beit
Hanoun

Gaza Wharf

Seaport

Gaza

Nahal Oz
Entry point for
liquid fuels

Nusseirat
Bureij RC

*Karni / Al-Muntar
Crossing*
Primary commercial
crossing (import & export)

Netivot

Maghazi

Deir
Al-Balah

Buffer
zone

ISRAEL

Buffer Zone
150 to 500 m buffer
imposed by the Israeli
forces. Movement is
restricted by frequent army
warning fire.

Khan
Younis

Northern No-Go Zone
Covering the former
northern settlement bloc,
movement in this area is
restricted to residents and
international organizations
since 28 December 2005.

EGYPT

Rafah

*Rafah Terminal
International Crossing*
Crossing point
for people

Airport

*Sufa / Al-Matar
Crossing*
Entry point predominantly for
aggregates and construction materials

*Kerem Shalom / Karm Abu Salem
International Cargo Crossing (located in Israel)*
Entry point for goods from Egypt

10 km

Palestinian Localities	Industrial Area	Minor Crossing Points
Former Israeli Settlement Blocs pre-2005 Disengagement	Philadelphia Corridor	Major Crossing Points
Palestinian Coastal Strip Cultivation (Al-Mawasi)	Palestinian Road	500 metre Buffer Zone
Greenhouse Zone	Israeli Road Link	150 metre Buffer Zone and Northern No-Go Zone
	Double Wire Fence with Watch Tower	

PREFACE

I'd ridden with the ambulances since Wednesday afternoon. In the darkness of early evening, we'd arrived at a residential tower block that was a scene of chaos, terrified people pouring out of its doors, having fled down endless stairs. Craning my neck, I could see the top storey was destroyed, and the next was on fire. The medic I was working with ran towards the apartment entrance, where someone thrust into his arms a baby girl of about 1, bleeding from the head. As we sped towards Al Shifa, she screamed, then slipped into unconsciousness, then woke a few seconds later to express her pain and outrage further. I passed bandages and cheered her on; the fact she kept waking to cry meant she had half a chance. We handed her in and went back to the scene. As we left the apartment building with the next injured resident, the ground rocked. Same building, second strike.

Returning to Al Quds hospital later, with the army getting ever closer, we realised that anyone who left the hospital again might not get back to it. I decided to stay. I couldn't think of anything worse than being on one side of an army line while the hospital was on the other. But it wasn't long anyway before the bosses of the medic teams instructed all but two of the ambulances to leave, go park up at Al Shifa hospital in the city centre, and answer calls from there, where their mobility and safety was more assured than in Tel al Howa. Al Quds retained two ambulances, and they were stationed at the front door. The hospital had to retain some emergency transport, even though it risked them being turned into the same burnt-out husks as the ambulances round the corner beside the evacuated Red Crescent Dispatch Centre.

By the early hours of Thursday morning, our world had shrunk to Al Quds hospital only. All else was darkness and explosions. Mobiles worked only intermittently. Some of the locals had taken shelter with us. Al Jazeera English had asked me if I could write something about what the current situation was like for pregnant women, and so I'd spent some of the evening downstairs in the obstetrics department, housed in the basement of the middle building, speaking to an obstetrician with the help of Raja, the prettiest nurse in Al Quds. I'd helped feed the triplets in their incubators. Finally, I'd joined some of the Disaster Team and the hospital's dietician to smoke on the front porch of the main building; the broken middle building we'd previously gone to for this now deemed too far away, though we continued to access obstetrics and A&E there via the basement route. Each explosion seemed closer. We rocked along with the ground and the buildings. It felt as if the end of the world was coming. In which case smoking *shisha* beside my friends seemed the right thing to do.

Once smoking was finished, if occurred to me that there was another sensible thing to do at this point, something I hadn't done for a while. Sleep. So I found one of the offices with a chair still free, and a blanket, and settled down amid snoring off-shift Disaster Team workers. The disaster was going to come right to us. All that was left to do now, was wait for it.

At some point in the early hours, an enormous explosion threw me out of sleep. I sat bolt upright, only somewhat awake, saying something very loudly that you should never say in Palestine, but then, strangely, lay down and went immediately back to sleep. I realise now, looking back, that what I was expecting was for the army to occupy the hospital. Nothing else was really registering. With all those explosions, my unconscious was playing some sort of game whereby every bang that I heard that didn't get me, didn't get *anyone*. Despite the daily evidence I'd seen of rubble where buildings had been, of body parts where people had been. Sometimes explosions came every few minutes. How could I bear to equate each one I heard with another death, another home gone? I guess I couldn't. Not till afterwards. Yet as I slept, all around us, Tel al Howa was burning, and that explosion that woke me was probably the first direct hit to the hospital. From this point, time becomes elastic.

1

DECEMBER 14, 2004–NOVEMBER 18, 2008

Breaking the Siege

It was a Jewish friend who first sent me to Palestine, in 2002. She and other long-term mates had returned with good reports of volunteering with the recently formed International Solidarity Movement, created by Israelis and Palestinians to invite internationals to support Palestinians in nonviolent struggle against Israeli occupation. It sounded creative, flexible, and accessible, and I decided to go and learn what I could.

ISM's work began with internationals accompanying Palestinians as they harvested their crops or cared for their sheep under regular attack from Israeli settlers, or attempted to get to work or school or hospital through humiliating army checkpoints. But it swiftly expanded to accompanying them in nonviolent resistance to Israel's new wall, the wall that was stealing land, olive groves, a village's water supply – or half the village – for Israel. Village after village faced up to the army, and year after year, an increasing number of us from all round the world saved up what we could, and went to stand beside these villagers.

DECEMBER 14, 2004

A soldier pulls out a tear gas canister and throws it amongst us – BANG – smoke. The *shebab* (teenage and young men) and children scatter shouting – they respond to everything in a fairly skittish way. Most of us grown ups try to stand our ground, or move calmly if we have to. But there are more bangs – sound grenades now mixed in with the gas – and more smoke, and people are shouting because you have to let those around you know when the soldiers are taking aim, when something is coming in your direction, when someone is hurt and needs help. And if you don't see these canisters thrown or fired then you don't see them till they land beside you or hit you, unless someone shouts.

At first you think it is ok because you can see the smoke, and it clears well on the hillside. But then you realise the white smoke is only part of it, the gas that affects you is invisible, you don't know it will get you till it does. I only get a taste of the burning of it, but others fall to the ground trying to catch their breath, unable to see. People crush onions and lemons in their hands, hand them to each other, to breathe in to trigger their lungs to start up again.

Trying to look in all directions at once, I see a soldier take aim at a Palestinian man only yards away, and throw a sound grenade directly at him. It explodes and he falls to the ground, he cries out and puts his hands to his head; four men run to carry him away. It is a long way to a road, and we are in the countryside, I don't know where the nearest ambulance might be. Soldiers keep aiming at them as they try to run up the hill.

Palestinians shout angrily at this direct attack on unarmed people, Israeli soldiers shout back. A woman stands in the middle of the crowd, berating the soldiers at the top of her voice. Someone near me says that she is shouting 'You shot my husband, my brother, my son, now I want to die here, on the land.' A younger woman tries to stay near her. Whenever I catch sight of her she is clutching the same rock in her hand, as if she wants to throw it but knows how pointless it will be, or that she isn't strong enough to throw it far enough, or maybe it just makes her feel safer somehow.

The tension has heightened and suddenly the soldiers are aiming their guns, about to shoot rubber-coated bullets – which also kill. Many voices call out, in rage and despair – all I understand is what us internationals are calling, variations along the lines of 'No-one is armed here!' 'Why are you doing this? How can you do this?' 'Please calm down!' and from the Israelis amongst us – *'Shalom, shalom!'*

We try to move to leave no Palestinians unguarded, but there are not so many of us. I put myself somewhere between two groups of villagers, glancing back and forth between them, and to the soldiers, one particularly who is aiming for various men on the other side of me and only has to pull the trigger.

My arms are outstretched, spread wide, palms up, briefly we all freeze. I face the soldiers, the Palestinians are behind me. 'Please don't do this,' I call to them. 'Please.' My knees are trembling, but what I feel is just intensity and focus, as if with my body and my voice I must and can somehow keep people from dying today…

After killing and injuring some of us, including Rachel Corrie and Tom Hurndall, and finding that didn't discourage ISM volunteers as might reasonably have been expected and also that it didn't go down too well internationally, it didn't take Israel long to invent the Blacklist.

DECEMBER 20, 2005

I am writing from my top bunk bed, here in Ben Gurion airport's detention cells. Vik (from Italy) and Michael (from South Africa, living in the UK) are next door. We were brought here some hours ago, when, not entirely to our surprise, Israeli Immigration refused the three of us entry for 'security reasons', an explanation they never feel the need to elaborate on.

I have a tendency to be optimistic despite evidence, so I was determinedly ignoring the fact that when I last came here, I was questioned for eight hours behind a door labelled *Ministry of Defence*. After all, this time we had our personal invitations to the International Nonviolence Conference in Bethlehem. How threatening could we be?

Upon disembarking, we followed our fellow passengers through the elegant new airport halls, fronted up to the Passport Counter, and handed in our passports. I looked back to offer Vik a smile – he had already been refused entry six months ago, so I knew he wouldn't be feeling so confident. But by the time I turned round again, several tall men in plain clothes had materialised in front of us. 'You're together?' asked one. 'Please come this way.'

The rest of the day was fairly predictable. Hours of questions such as 'What places have you been to in the West Bank? What Palestinians do you know?' (we were happy to answer the first kind, and unwilling to answer the second) interspersed with hours of waiting in a corner, plus a thorough bag and body search. As the man questioning me snapped several pictures, he offered a smile so false it put my teeth on edge, saying, 'I'm sure you can clear it up for us, but you know, for some reason, the authorities seem to have some concerns about you.'

I began to wonder if this interrogation was all a sham, and, when he asked me to tell him about my presence on an occasion when the Israeli Army had opened live fire on internationals who were retreating with their hands in the air, wounding many, I experimented by replying, 'I don't really like to talk about that.'

'Oh well, doesn't matter,' he said breezily. At that point I realised they'd never considered letting us in.

So here we are in our cells, ostensibly awaiting the next flight out. Plan A was to enter with no trouble and go to the Conference, but we do have a Plan B. Although we have not been permitted to call our consulates or a lawyer, friends notified our lawyer. She comes to see us, and explains that she will get an order allowing us to stay for a court hearing by tomorrow afternoon, but that the authorities will try to get us back on a plane before that if they can.

So I'm curled up under a grey wool blanket, but dressed, boots and all. I suspect they will come in the early hours of the morning, and I don't want to be at a disadvantage. I am sharing the four-bed cell with a Russian woman, Jana. We ascertained that the only Russian word I know is *chai* – tea – (it's the same in Arabic), so we've been communicating by smiles and gestures. I wonder what her story is. Using her fingers, she's told me that she has been in this cell for ten days. Since we are not allowed to make phone calls, how do other people ask for help? What if they have no-one on the outside to help them? The fluorescent lights stay on all night.

DECEMBER 21, 2005

They come at 4am, two guards; the rattle of the keys wakes me. 'Get ready for the plane,' they say. I sit up, and hook my boots under the bedframe. 'I'm not willing to go on the plane,' I reply. 'I want to stay and go to court.' They look a bit startled by this. I have a feeling most of the women who end up here – for example foreign workers whose visas have run out – generally do as they're told. Another, higher-up officer appears; he shouts at me, 'It is not up to you! You have no choice! You have five minutes!' then stomps off. Next door, I hear Michael and Vik getting similarly shouted at. In my head I feel calm, but my body is shaking. I lie tensely waiting for time to pass. Each time I nod off, I jerk awake at any noise. An hour later, I realise they're not coming back.

I spend the day reading. At 4pm, I hear shouting from next door. I press my ear to the glass window onto the corridor, trying to understand what is going on.

It is not till days later that I hear the background to what happens next. What I can't see is a group of police entering Michael and Vik's s cell and announcing they will be removed by force, starting with Michael, who Vik immediately gets a grip on. Michael and Vik repeatedly ask to speak to our lawyer, stating that she has obtained a permit for us to take our case to court. When Vik demands to call the Italian consulate, a policeman knees him in the groin. Once they have Vik (who has a heart condition) on the ground, he clings to the bed frame, so they start punching and kicking him. All I can hear is Vik shouting in pain, and I cannot understand what is happening, until the police drag him through his cell door and into the corridor where I can see him.

Vik is on his stomach on the ground, his hands cuffed and pushed high behind his back, with six police on top of him, apparently without any plan other than to force him into submission. Unable to see, he clings to anything he can grab – chairs, then a picture that falls to the ground, where the glass front smashes so shards cover the floor. An attempt is made to sweep them out of the way, but enough remain that blood quickly appears on the floor. Vik has been shouting in Italian, but finally manages in English – 'I can't breathe! I'm sick! I need a doctor!'

I am shouting too, helpless behind my door. Despite my pleas, the violence ends only as it dawns on the police that Vik really needs to go to hospital. He cannot stand or walk, so they put him on an office chair with wheels and transport him away from my line of vision.

When next I see him, days later, Vik tells me that he believed he was having a heart attack (his medication had been confiscated on arrival in the cells) but this turned out to be pain from torn chest muscles. He spent several hours in the hospital being treated for shock, then was returned to the cells to spend the remainder of the week in CCTV-monitored solitary confinement.

DECEMBER 22, 2005

Today a young American woman arrives. It's great to be able to talk to someone again. She is trying to visit relatives in Bethlehem, where she was born, but left when she was 29 days old. She has a US passport, but the Israeli embassy back home advised her to bring her old Palestine papers as well. Despite being advised in advance that she would be treated as an American citizen, not a Palestinian, she has been refused entry.

'Can we open that door from our side?' she asks me.

'Nope,' I say.

'And can we put this light out when we want?' she tries.

I shake my head.

There is a thoughtful pause.

'I'm in a cell, aren't I,' she says.

'Oh yes,' I reply.

Tonight I find myself staring at the false ceiling from a sort of James Bond point of view. I could lift out a piece and climb in there. I spend some time trying to think of what I would do after that.

DECEMBER 25, 2005

Today Jana and I have two Christmas presents. The first is Natalia, a young Bulgarian student with a bright smile who speaks both our languages. She was here to visit Israeli friends, but back home she studied Arabic, and she had some Arabic friends' names on her phone, so she has ended up in detention instead.

Then later today, the rattle of keys is followed by a soft Scottish voice asking cheerfully, 'Is there a bed free in here?' It is Theresa, another ISM volunteer who was also hoping to attend the Nonviolence Conference. She has brought a whole bunch of Christmassy chocolate coins in gold paper, which makes us all happy. When we see Michael in the corridor outside having a smoke break, we slide some under the door to him. Theresa says Vik was holding notes up to the window when she was being processed earlier. 'What did they say?' I ask, still worried he's got broken bones. 'That there will be an eclipse tonight,' she replies. This makes me fall about laughing. Even in prison Vik manages to hold on to the poetry in life!

A young guard, working to fund his studies, lets me out with Theresa for her smoke break today. He responds to our descriptions of the Israeli army regularly firing upon unarmed men, women, and children, with the disbelief I often hear from Israelis uninvolved in the peace movement. 'No,' he says, 'Jewish people wouldn't do that.' 'I have seen it, many times; it is an accepted policy,' I tell him. 'No,' he repeats, 'there must have been some mistake, or you didn't understand.'

What I find interesting is that when people respond in this way, they don't try to suggest that I am lying, but they never ask for any more details. It is simply that it does not fit with what they wish to believe about their country. I wish I knew how to present the truth so it could be heard by young Israelis like my guard. But it's like I'm trying to tell him the earth is flat.

DECEMBER 27, 2005

Today we go to court. I hug Theresa goodbye and am taken to join Michael and Vik, handcuffed together. I am so relieved to see them – I've been able to wave at Michael, a single dad in his fifties, through our cell windows, but have seen nothing of Vik since he was on the floor bleeding. Being together and seeing the outside world through the van windows makes us feel strangely festive. Even the guards are cheerful. 'We'll give you a tour of Tel Aviv – five shekels!' they joke.

The court case is entirely in Hebrew; when Israeli friends try to whisper translations they are told to stop. An hour of 'secret evidence' about us is included, which neither we nor our lawyer are allowed to hear. As the judge states his conclusion, I watch the faces of everyone in the court room. The minutes stretch out; even our friends haven't given us any sign. Finally, one turns and shakes her head.

Italian journalists hover, waiting to interview Vik, as our lawyer comes over to give a quick summary. The judge's reason for upholding the refusal of our entry is that we have all, in the past, been with Palestinians holding non-violent demonstrations against their land being stolen by the Separation Wall, in the face of armed response by Israel.

In the middle of the night, I find myself sobbing into my sleeping bag, trying not to wake Theresa. I'm a privileged white Westerner, and nobody ever before has stopped me from going where I need to go. God knows what it is like to be a Palestinian for whom freedom of movement, or being with all your family, is just something to dream about.

DECEMBER 28, 2005

I leave Theresa with my books – she awaits her own court case. Our guards take us to the plane and march ahead with the passports, up the ramp. Vik and I pause simultaneously, wanting to keep our feet on this ground. We are still separated by concrete, country and distance from the place we want to be. But if we turned and walked from here, however long it took, we could get to Palestine. I know, because I have stood in Budrus – the village that successfully pushed the Separation Wall back from its land – and seen the lights of Tel Aviv.

But if there's one thing I've tried to learn from Palestinians, it's never to give up. So it's time now to go home, and figure out what comes next.

What came next was a whole lot of work over email with a bunch of people I'd never met, who were mostly in the same (blacklisted) boat as me – followed by an extraordinary day in August 2008, when we really were in the same boat – or rather, boats. Me and Vik and Theresa, and 41 others from all over the world.

AUGUST 21, 2008

I will always be grateful to Derek, because the night before the original Free Gaza sailing from Cyprus, when my sanity was hanging by a thread after two years of working on this whole crazy project, he persuaded me to spend the entire night dancing in a strange silver-decored bar. Something to do with Irish charm and First Mate's authority. We arrived back to the port just in time to sail. Without his intervention I might have drowned myself from sheer fatigue and missed the whole thing.

The preceding weeks had given me great joy, but had also been overwhelming and exhausting, with delay upon delay and everyone's tempers frayed. Most participants were arriving to Cyprus, others of us were elsewhere, helping the experts with the boat logistics. The Israeli press published speculative articles...

According to the Free Gaza Movement's website, the activists will include a Holocaust survivor, [and] a survivor of the Palestinian Nakba... the plan is for the boat to enter

Gaza's territorial waters, and more specifically, the 'special security zone' that the Israeli Navy has declared off-limits to all boats... Israel is still trying to discover the ship's exact identity... it is also trying to decide how to respond. One option that has been raised in official discussions is to simply allow the ship to reach Gaza, thereby foiling the organizers' apparent desire for a clash.[1]

(Ooh, go on – foil us, foil us!)

On July 29 we held a press conference in Athens, announcing the boats' presence at an unspecified location in Greece, and stating: 'From today, any attempt to damage the project will be considered an act of aggression against a nonviolent international human rights mission.'

Our only precursor of which we were aware, the Palestinian-led 1988 Ship of Return project, had its boat engine blown up and three organisers assassinated. I'm sure I wasn't

1.1 Vik helps the Greeks prepare the *Free Gaza*, while she and the *Liberty* are still hidden among the islands.

Sharyn Lock

the only one thinking, as I made lots of boat-related lists and plans, that the organisers of that attempt must have been making similar lists and plans, with similar hope in their hearts.

Without the stress, my days on a sunny car-free island, doing unskilled painting and sanding on a lovely fishing boat under the instruction of the awesomely hard-working Greeks, would have been paradise. At the end of each long, hot day of boat and computer work, there was the bright sea to dive into, and Vik to drink *mojitos* with as we sat in the port at night, watching over our boat and hardly daring to blink.

I didn't want to be assassinated, and found it hard to imagine anyone would bother. I did, however, think that once we finally set sail to Gaza, Israel would bomb our boats. I thought we were going to die. Under the Mediterranean sun, under a sky full of stars, Vik and I thought we were probably living our last days. And we thought that if it had to happen, it would be a pretty good way to go.

1.2   The *Liberty*, taken from the *Free Gaza*, on the morning of August 23, hours before we arrived at Gaza.

Sharyn Lock

AUGUST 24

How can I possibly begin to coherently write anything of the last 24 hours? I can't even comprehend any of it right now, let alone communicate it. It'll just have to come in scraps of thoughts...

Yvonne and I are sitting here, trying to think of the date yesterday.

'We've made history and neither of us even know what day we did it on,' says Yvonne. 'Just as well it wasn't us running the Battle of Hastings. We'd be saying – 1063 was it? 1065 maybe?'

We've now agreed it was August 23 yesterday, and I am very much hoping that finally gets me into the Housmans Peace Diary, without actually dying.

We left Cyprus on August 22, in the morning, and were very lucky to have two slightly cloudy days, because normally there simply wasn't enough shade for 25 people above deck on the *Free Gaza*, and below was steaming hot. The sea was good in sailors' terms, but enough so that most people were a little sick and about eight very sick.

Acting as medic with former nurse Kathy turned out to be the perfect job for me. I spend most of the night feeling a little queasy unless lying flat on the deck, but one of my comrades was so ill all night that we had to keep rehydrating her at 15 minute intervals. I simply lay beside her, drowsing in between doses, observing our fantastic crew as they stepped over me and my patient to keep *Free Gaza* going through the night in two hour watches. The sense of being in a great randomly rocking cradle was intensified by watching the unchanging stars above.

Sometimes I could get up for a little while and gaze at the horizon, sea-edged in all directions, watching lights of occasional other ships (which always unnerved us a little) as well as the red port light of the *Liberty* moving parallel with us. During the day, the sun had been harsh, but on the sea at night there is just beauty.

Channel 16 is the emergency radio channel which must always be kept unobstructed, but ever since sailing from Greece there had been strange messages in Hebrew, Arabic music played at us, etc. Tonight, someone was just repeating: 'They're lost. They're lost.'

For long stretches at a time, our two boats couldn't contact each other, though we could see each other's lights. Never rely on technology – satellite phones, radios, expensive internet and video streaming – the last apparently sabotaged from a distance before we even set sail, though it functioned a little sometimes. The rest entirely stopped working on both boats shortly after the 'they're lost' broadcast. We were no longer able to use even the normal sea communications systems for SOS messages. We heard later that the Greek government, wondering how the MP they had sent with us was doing, had tried every method to contact us and eventually decided we must have sunk.

Before the comms systems went down, however, we'd heard that the media coverage had taken off, and that the Arab League had announced its support of us, and stated that Israel must act in every way to protect our peaceful mission. Then there was silence.

But we had two secret weapons: (1) Our walkie-talkies, too low tech to be sabotaged. They worked at least some of the time, and then we could talk between the two boats. (2) Mr Ramattan[2] and Mr Al Jazeera – our captive journalists – had a functioning satellite phone. On this we put out a press release announcing the apparent sabotage, calling particularly on the Greek government to protest this as we were sailing under the Greek flag (actually we were sailing under about 50 flags, including a Free Leonard Peltier one; I wished I'd brought the Aboriginal one I was given last time I was in Australia).

Morning was a blessing. Everyone cheered up, I felt fine again, the sick people attempted some dry Greek bread, the undefeatedly cheerful Lauren stopped juggling walkie-talkies and made yet another round of tea (I apologise for thinking her most useful role was being related to Tony Blair). The single working phone began ringing and didn't stop – Musheir giving interviews in Arabic, Vik in Italian, Jeff in Hebrew. We began to put up more flags. Conflicting messages came in about whether a media boat was coming from Israel to try to meet up with us. We kept grabbing passing crew and asking them – how many hours now left of international waters? Two, one. And then, we got a call from an Israeli journalist.

'The Foreign Minister has just stated, "We are not going to stop the boats."'

We weren't going to prison. Vik wasn't going to be climbing the mast and refusing to come down. I wasn't going to be shot for refusing to co-operate with the Israeli navy. We weren't going to get to eat our siege supply of stuffed vineleaves. Lauren wasn't going to get to sing 'Israeli men' to the tune of *It's Raining Men* as we were boarded, which was just as well, since we hadn't worked out the dance routine yet. None of that was happening. The impossible was happening. We were going to get to Gaza.

AUGUST 26

...So there we were, with First Mate Derek shouting at us to tidy up our boat for its imminent achievement of the impossible. We lurched about, picking up roll mats and empty water bottles, and then putting them down again to go and stand in the prow, gazing at a hazy horizon. Derek climbed the mast. I don't know how much time passed; all I was doing was beaming at everybody in turn. Then we heard Derek shout:

'LAND HO!'

I couldn't see a thing but we all began to cheer.

'Do it again for the camera,' said Mr Al Jazeera.

'LAND HO!' shouted Derek again.

'Didn't quite get that – '

'LAND – '

I looked for Mr Ramattan, hoping for the sake of Derek's voice that he was filming too. But Mr Ramattan was collapsed in the lifeboat, sobbing out a lifetime of Palestinian tears.

1.3   One of many fishing boats, overflowing with Palestinians as they welcome the *Free Gaza* and the *Liberty* arriving at Gaza port.

Sharyn Lock

Richard Falk, UN Special Rapporteur on Human Rights in the Occupied Palestinian Territories:

The landing of two wooden boats carrying 44 human rights activists in Gaza is an important symbolic victory. This non-violent initiative of the Free Gaza Movement focused attention around the world on the stark reality that the 1.5 million residents of Gaza have endured a punitive siege for more than a year. This siege is a form of collective punishment that constitutes a massive violation of Article 33 of the Fourth Geneva Convention.

The siege, the coastal blockade, and overflights by Israeli aircraft, all bear witness to the fact that, despite Israel's claimed 'disengagement' in 2005, these realities on the ground establish that Gaza remains under Israeli occupation, and as a result Israel remains legally responsible for protecting the human rights of its civilian population.

By severely restricting the entry of food, fuel, and medicine, the economic and social rights of the people of Gaza have been systematically violated... above all, what is being tested is whether the imaginative engagement of dedicated private citizens can influence the struggle of a beleaguered people for basic human rights, and whether their courage and commitment can awaken the conscience of humanity to an unfolding tragedy.

Musheir El-Farra, boat passenger, British resident, born in Khan Younis, Gaza:

For the first time in my life, I went to Gaza without being humiliated, without having to ask Israel for permission. We did it. We finally did it. And now others must join us and do it as well.

The boats made the return journey the following week, carrying Palestinians who needed to leave and most of the original passengers, who were dazed by a week of intensive viewing of the siege's miseries while being unwillingly treated like film stars, but determined to go home and work on the next journey. Some of us stayed; seven experienced ISMers gladly meeting up with Fida, Gaza's old ISM co-ordinator, to plot the international accompanying of fishermen, and another four of us planning to leave later on the upcoming Rafah border open day, when we understood that foreign passport holders would be allowed through.

I know now how naïve that was. The Egyptian border official who took our passports smiled at us, foreigners foolishly believing in some sort of functional system, and said with relish, 'You came on the Free Gaza boats. You are not allowed into Egypt.'

A diplomatic argument ensued, involving a range of consulates and politicians. Faxes and emails flew. Days passed. The deadline by which I had to turn up for my midwifery degree in England loomed.

Meanwhile, I went fishing.

Gaza's fishermen

According to Nizar Ayash, director of Gaza's Fishing Syndicate, there are over 3,000 registered fishermen in Gaza, and 40,000 people whose livelihoods depend on the industry. Most fishing is done by small to medium sized boats, catching bream and sardines.

During the 1990s an area extending 20 miles from the Gazan coast was fished under the provisions of the Oslo Accords, with a narrow no-fish zone at the edges of this, bordering Israeli and Egyptian territorial waters.

But attacks on Gaza fishermen by Israeli naval vessels became routine from the beginning of the Second Intifada in 2000, and were apparently stepped up after the kidnapping of Gilad Shalit in 2006. Some commentators have also linked them to the opening up of the Gaza gas field from 1999 to 2000.

Fishermen have been killed, wounded or arrested and nets, boats and other equipment damaged, stolen or destroyed. According to the Ministry of Agriculture, the attacks cost the industry $16.6 million between 2000 and 2008, and between 2000 and April 2009 16 fishermen were killed and over 200 injured.

Even during 'normal' periods fishing was restricted to an area up to six miles from the Gazan coast and boats routinely targeted from three miles offshore, with reports of attacks taking place just yards from the beach. The main shoals of fish on which the industry depends are found ten or more miles offshore. The fishing industry has also been affected by raw sewage being dumped in the Mediterranean due to the destruction of Gaza's sanitation systems.

In 2007, Israeli human rights NGO B'Tselem commented: 'In September 2005, Israel completed its Gaza disengagement plan and declared the end of the military government in the Gaza Strip. It is not clear, therefore, on what authority Israel forbids sailing off the Gaza coast, or what is the legal basis for detaining the fishermen, who are no longer subject, according to Israel 's contention, to its control.'

References: B'Tselem, 'IDF prohibits fishing off Gaza coast and abuse fishermen', February 2007; David Schermerhorn, 'Timeline of Gaza Marine Zone, Fishermen and Natural Gas Deposits', April 2009, www.globalresearch.ca

SEPTEMBER 11

An Israeli gunboat actually rammed one of the fishing boats today. It 'smashed through the upper hull of the fishing boat, careened over the top, and landed on the other side', making it a wonder no-one was killed. None of the internationals were there – perhaps the point. Apparently the gunboat itself was quite badly damaged, with some soldiers ending up overboard. The fishermen have speculated that the gunboat didn't realise the flimsy looking wooden cabin of the fishing boats hid a solid metal framework![3]

The last day I went out fishing, the Israeli gunboats shot around us for a while in the morning, threatening in Arabic over the megaphone to arrest the fishermen and take them to Israel, which happens constantly, or to start shooting directly at the boat. But they didn't. They actually went and sat on the horizon for most of the day, after announcing more politely in English: 'This is a closed area, you must leave.'

Jenny announced back to them over Channel 16 that these were Palestinian waters, over which they had no jurisdiction, that they were firing on unarmed people, and that they were being filmed.

As the sun set, the sea turned silver, and the fishermen served up the day's catch to break the Ramadan fast, our gunboat came back for a special Ramadan drive-by shooting before heading home – the flash of automatic fire drawing a line towards the prow where I was filming and wondering if they were going to stop when they reached me and the boat. They did, to begin again at the other end of the boat, and followed it up with a few explosion type things. Then they went home for their dinner too, we presume, and we ate our fried fish. Our first catches were small, but the last one very big, so the fishermen were happy.

SEPTEMBER 17

Free Gaza press release:

Italian human rights monitor injured by Israeli Navy off Gaza coast
An Italian human rights worker was injured today by the Israeli navy, while monitoring human rights abuses against Palestinian fishermen off the coast of the Gaza Strip.

Vittorio Arrigoni was hit by flying glass when the Israeli navy used a high-powered water cannon against the unarmed boats. The water cannon smashed the glass surrounding the steering section of the boat, with shards lacerating Arrigoni's back. He was taken to hospital immediately upon reaching shore, requiring stitches.

1.4   An Israeli gunboat attacks a Palestinian fishing boat with water cannon, autumn 2008.
Eva Bartlett

SEPTEMBER 23

Last week, when I finally extracted myself from the Rafah border a month after I first began trying to leave, was pretty stressful, but at least I didn't end up with ten stitches. Vik is doing fine, a little sheepish about all the fuss, but glad it was him and not one of his fishermen friends, to whom the media would have paid no attention. The hospital didn't let me watch him getting stitched up – 'in case I fainted'. How insulted am I? Water cannon are another weapon the Israeli gunboats commonly use on the fishermen, and the ISMers have since reported that the water they are getting soaked with now is foul, making everyone sick. It either contains some extremely dodgy chemicals or the contents of the gunboat's sewage tank. And they've been documenting that the gunboats actually shoot at people on the *shore* sometimes.

NOVEMBER 18

Free Gaza press release:

Urgent: Kidnapped by the Israeli Navy
Fourteen Palestinian fishermen, along with three internationals, have been kidnapped out of Palestinian waters by the Israeli Navy. They were fishing seven miles off the coast of Deir al Balah, clearly in Gaza waters.

The fishermen and international human rights observers were transferred from three separate boats to Israeli warships. Other Palestinian fishermen reported that the three boats were seen being taken north by the Israeli Navy.

The three internationals are Andrew Muncie from Scotland, Darlene Wallach from the United States, and Viktor Arrigoni from Italy… Fellow activists have been unable to establish contact with the HROs or with the fishermen since they were abducted.

An Italian consulate guy has managed to see Vik, who's ok. So is Andrew, and it seems they're refusing deportation until the fishermen are released, as expected. No-one has been able to find out anything about Darlene, as the US consulate are saying she 'didn't sign the privacy waiver'...even though we have a copy of it.

The fishermen were released the following day; Darlene, Vik and Andrew went on hunger strike to demand the release of the boats. After a grim few days of punishments such as isolation and being put in flea infested cells, they were deported. A week later, the ISM lawyers successfully extracted the boats from Israel's clutches. The GPS systems had been stolen.

It was nearly December, and I was ready to head back, my University having kindly deferred my place. I remembered the last text I had sent to Vik as I left Gaza in September: 'Take care out fishing... but if you get taken to Israel, we can fight our way back to Gaza together.'

Since our first journey, *Free Gaza* had successfully made the crossing twice more, carrying Israeli and Palestinian Members of Parliament including Mustafa Barghouti; eleven of the 53 members of the European Parliamentary delegation that was refused entry by land at the Rafah border, including UK MP Clare Short, former MP Baroness Jenny Tong, Nobel Peace Prize winner Mairead Maguire and Italian opera singer Joe Felucci – as well as more medical supplies. And Palestinians with study visas or needing medical treatment had been brought out.

The project had also been praised by the President of the UN, Miguel d'Escoto Brockmann, at the UN General Assembly:

Gandhi's and King's successors in the twenty-first century have carried out further experiments in the power of nonviolent truth to achieve justice and peace in every corner of the world – including, in the last two months, Gaza. The Free Gaza Movement has succeeded in breaking the siege of Gaza by nonviolent direct action. After sailing from Cyprus, 44 activists from 17 countries landed their two small wooden boats at Gaza Port on August 23, 2008, where a beleaguered people welcomed them. This nonviolent initiative allowed Palestinians to enter and leave their own country freely for the first time in over 60 years.[4]

But none of us, not even the President of the UN, could have imagined what the next stage of this 'unfolding tragedy' was going to be.

2
DECEMBER 3–DECEMBER 26, 2008

Escalating Violence

Arriving in Cyprus on December 3, I am given news of the possible delay of Free Gaza journey no. 4. By the day of sailing, the Qatari charity who were providing the VIP presence and the cargo have changed their minds. We think the Israeli government is pressuring them to send their cargo of cancer drugs to Gaza via the Israeli port of Ashdod.

Free Gaza folks are both frustrated at the sudden withdrawal of this journey's cargo and the 'important people' that would hopefully protect the rest of us a little, and massively sceptical about the success of any other options.

'So…who would like to try to write a press release saying our publicised delegation has pulled out, and as a result we don't have a cargo, yet with an upbeat tone about how we hope to find some more VIPs and cargo in the next 48 hours and go on Tuesday, but without actually committing us to anything?' asks Ramzi.

Surrounded by laptops, empty pizza boxes, and half packed bags, everyone is worried. Just a few days ago on December 2, a Libyan ship attempting to bring Gaza 3,000 tonnes of food aid and medicine, plus a crew of Scouts (yes, Scouts) was stopped by the Israeli navy. On December 6, a Palestinian/Israeli boat with Knesset members aboard (including Palestinians holding Israeli citizenship) will try to make the journey from Israel to Gaza by sea, but no-one likes their chances. It is illegal under Israeli law for Israelis to enter Gaza, making it extremely difficult for Israelis and Palestinians to meet each other as individuals. *Free Gaza* passenger Jeff Halper was arrested on his return to Israel in August.

A couple of days and many phone calls later, we finally sail with the swiftly organised Academic Delegation – aka Drs Mike Cushman and Jonathan Rosenhead from the London School of Economics, who have upped and joined us at no notice, to visit Gaza's universities and escort out some of the 700 Gaza students trying to get to their scholarships elsewhere in the world.

Also we are bringing a surgeon, some journalists, Nasser – a Palestinian man who is unable to get home any other way – and a medical cargo donated by the Qatari charity despite the fact they aren't coming along themselves.

But the Free Gaza board has decided Vik can't go this time. Without politically important types onboard, they are worried Israel may use the excuse that they recently removed Vik from Gaza and thus pretend some legitimacy in stopping the boat. Another trip is scheduled in a few weeks and they promise he can be on that. A gloomy Vik retreats to Cyprus limbo in Jenny and Derek's spare room, to internet roulette and sleep. His Gaza friends, apartment, and work await him, and I think, like me, he always fears the worst. If this boat turns out to be the last successful trip, he will be stuck outside Palestine, again.

He and Derek and I have a reprise of our August 21st night out; we even manage to find the strange silver nightclub again. The snug little *Dignity* sails the next day – with my old friend Ewa (British-Polish activist and journalist) among the passengers, coming to share the Free Gaza liaison role with Irish activist Caoimhe, who caught the second Free Gaza boat over in October; the *Dignity*'s maiden voyage. I haven't seen Caoimhe since the Lebanese army's attack on the Palestinian refugee camp Nahr Al Bared, in 2007.

DECEMBER 9

There's me breathing a sigh of relief that we had a proper doctor on board for any emergencies – and instead I spent my night checking up on her as she suffered the worst seasickness of us all. But the good ship *Dignity* had carpet! And a bidet! And a toaster! And patio doors! The boxes of baby milk and medicine got the best bedroom though.

Perpetual first mate Derek wore a shirt that read 'I've been to Gaza and back – with Dignity'. Anyone who has had to face the Rafah border understands the depth of meaning that carries.

That boat goes fast. It's a bit like a computer game. If you press the right buttons, you can let her get on with it by herself.

Nasser hasn't seen his family in four years. Many times he has fought the Rafah border and failed to get home. He perched on the front of the boat for the last few miles, clutching his flag, looking for his children. Can you imagine what it was like to see his family waiting; see their faces as they recognised him? After four years, you might be afraid you wouldn't know your own father.

I'm back in Gaza. Tomorrow is International Human Rights Day.

The original Qatari cargo never made it to Gaza via Ashdod port. And Israel blocked the Knesset boat and arrested three of the participating Knesset members.[1]

DECEMBER 12

As I type, on the other side of the sea, eleven newly disembarked young students are going through customs in Cyprus, just in time to take up their nearly expired study visas in various parts of the world. We wondered if Israel would attempt to interfere with us taking out a boatload of young men – the Israeli army traditionally seems to consider being a young Palestinian man an arrestable offence in itself.

The six month ceasefire is officially up in only a few days, so international voices may be vital soon. Though many people believe both sides will work for an extension. In the last few days, the UN's Special Rapporteur for the Occupied Territories, Richard Falk, wrote:

> Protective action must be taken immediately to offset the persisting and wide-ranging violations of the fundamental human right to life, and in view of the emergency situation that is producing a humanitarian catastrophe that is unfolding day by day... it would seem mandatory for the International Criminal Court to investigate the situation, and determine whether the Israeli civilian leaders and military commanders responsible for the Gaza siege should be indicted and prosecuted for violations of international criminal law. As Abu Zayd[2] has declared, 'This is a humanitarian crisis deliberately imposed by political actors.'

It should be noted that the situation worsened in recent days due to the breakdown of a truce between Hamas and Israel that had been observed for several months by both sides. The truce was maintained by Hamas despite the failure of Israel to fulfill its obligation under the agreement to improve the living conditions of the people of Gaza.

The recent upsurge of violence occurred after an Israeli incursion that killed several alleged Palestinian militants within Gaza. It is a criminal violation of international law for elements of Hamas or anyone else to fire rockets at Israeli towns regardless of provocation, but such Palestinian behavior does not legalize Israel's imposition of collective punishment of a life- and health-threatening character on the people of Gaza, and should not distract the UN or international society from discharging their fundamental moral and legal duty to render protection to the Palestinian people.[3]

DECEMBER 15

In the darkness...no-one can see if the kettle is boiling.

The strongest light I can see tonight is the full moon. There has been no power all day, and none has arrived with the startlingly sudden darkness.

Today I went to meet with Dr Yousef, the CEO of the Union of Health Work Committees, an NGO begun by volunteers 23 years ago, which looks after the health of the increasing number of people who can't afford to pay. He is a kind man who has had me proof-reading his reports on Gaza's health situation, elegantly worded documents that somehow combine increasing desperation with dignity. Eventually I hope to find a practical voluntary role in one of their local clinics, and find out lots of stories of life under siege. We are waiting to find out if accompanying the fishermen will continue also.

I went to visit my friend Moh today. At the moment, everyone asks everyone else solicitously – 'you have gas?' Moh pointed out that his gas canister is covered in mud, a legacy of its journey through the tunnels from Egypt which keep besieged Gaza supplied with such necessities

– expensively, both in terms of price and lives lost. Cooking-gas is apparently not one of the things Israel feels people should have. A journalist supporting himself only, Moh paid the equivalent of £65 for it, which most families couldn't possibly afford. In the UK, I'd pay about £15. Boiled eggs are my most common meal right now, but in deference to the gas situation, they are *soft* boiled eggs...

Remember that strongly worded article from Richard Falk at the UN? So did Israel. He was arriving for West Bank meetings, but they refused him entry, detained him in the same prison I spent time in in 2005, then deported him to Switzerland for good measure. I wonder how he feels about boats?

DECEMBER 16

I was hanging out at the Union of Health Work Committees today, slowly getting the hang of setting up a WordPress blog, when Dr Yousef came and asked me something beginning with 'Do you want to come to...?'

I'm often a bit unclear on what's going on around me here, but I tend to just say yes to questions that start like that. Whatever I've agreed to, there's always a good chance friendly people and sweet minty tea will be involved, and that's all I need to know.

It turned out that he and some of the other senior figures were going to drop in on three simultaneous free clinics, two in Bureij refugee camp and one in nearby Nuseirat. The UHWC runs three or four of these days a month, in different places round Gaza. The first offered a dentist, who was seeing 24 patients that day, and a skin specialist, who had 29 people booked. A walk away, lots of small children were part of the queue waiting on darkened (no electricity) concrete stairs to visit a paediatrician, an orthopaedic specialist, and a GP. Medicines were also being dispensed. It was 2pm, and already 250 patients had been seen.

Despite the busyness, they managed to deliver a hot lunch which we ate speedily, Dr Yousef threatening to send me to observe the multiple circumcisions going on. This was something I did in fact watch in the Al Shifa Clinic in Beddawi, Lebanon, when I was volunteering there. Dr Tawfiq had told me then that his belief is, if the procedure is done very early on, the babies don't appear to experience pain. And in fact the tiny little boy I observed didn't cry, although he did look slightly surprised (as you might). For this reason, Dr Tawfiq thought it important that there be no delay to the process, that eight days after birth, for example, was too old. I wondered how many of the babies here in Bureij had had to wait until the free clinic day, with there simply being no money for it otherwise.

Bureij camp houses 40,000 refugees, who originally lost their homes in the area that is now Tel Aviv's Ben Gurion airport. On many corners of the camp's ramshackle streets impromptu stalls had appeared, selling large water bottles refilled with fuel, for generators and lighting, fuel which once again has probably come from Egypt through the tunnels under the city of Rafah.

In Nuseirat, the Al Khairia medical centre is a light modern building, funded by Germany. It is managed by Dr Suzanne, who wears sunglasses pushing back her hair rather than a headscarf. It includes health education services, and on the fourth floor, Dr Yousef hopes to one day install an eye clinic. Cataracts, he explains, can be treated swiftly by new technology. 'But,' he returns to current reality, 'all funding right now is just spent on keeping the basics going, on handling the large scale health care emergency we are facing. That's all we can do in our situation. Just try to keep going.'

DECEMBER 18

I've never been to visit the house of a martyr[4] before, not someone who was alive the day before. On the way I find out this is one of the times that covering my head is non-negotiable, as a sign of respect, but I can do it old-fashioned Palestinian style rather than Islamic *hijab* style; my hair doesn't have to be hidden, it's more symbolic than anything.

All my instincts are against intruding into the home of seven children who no longer have the father they had this time yesterday. But here such a visit is a strong tradition and sign of respect. And we are showing this family that people 'outside' do care what has happened and are mourning their loss.

When we arrive to the house on the edge of Jabalia camp, the men are gathering outside, and the women inside the neighbouring house, where we join them. A young woman reads the Koran, with the lovely woodwind-like timbre I have heard from other Palestinian girls reciting in public.

Salah Oakal was 46, his wife must be in her late thirties. She wears an expression of stunned patience, sitting quietly in the middle of the row of women, accepting condolences from everyone as they arrive to sit with her. Another relative, an elderly woman wearing the traditional black dress with intricate purple embroidery and a snowy white headcovering, tells Canadian activist Eva and me the story; I can't understand more than a few words, but I don't think that is important for her, she just needs to tell it.

We go to the family's house across the street. These folks didn't have much to start with. Crumbling concrete walls, only a couple of rooms, bedding, that's pretty much it. All their crockery is now smashed on the floor of the kitchen, and some of the wall is missing. The wall of the childrens' room is entirely gone, replaced for now by a blanket. Three of them were inside at the time. And the 'ground to ground' missile didn't even hit the house; it's in a big hole just outside. Salah went out to water the trees, everyone explains, just to water the little trees right outside the house. He was only out for a moment. He was going to come back in to help prepare the dinner.

And after the impact, they couldn't find him. They looked for an hour in the dark. They couldn't find him because there was no electricity.

They couldn't find him because the impact had lifted him up and thrown him down. And, as they discovered when the ambulance arrived with headlights, they couldn't find him because he was now in three pieces.

'Did you hear any firing in this area?' Eva asks. 'From Palestinians? Because you know that's what Israel will say.' Everyone shakes their heads blankly.

Next door, we visit Eva's friends. Bits of their house are missing too, pieces out of the childrens' room once again; the children apparently protected by the right thing falling on them rather than the wrong thing. *Alhumdulallah*, thanks be to God, says everyone. Eva arrived in November with the third Free Gaza boat, but she began making Gaza friends even before that, in Egypt, during a futile wait for access through the Rafah border.

I am not sure exactly why the headcovering goes with visiting a martyr's house. Maybe it's because the family left behind with little to comfort them need to feel that God is closer by than usual, and it's only fair enough we should be dressed respectfully while he's around.

Neither Eva nor I ever really established a consistent policy on wearing headscarves. For mourning houses only, all of us women wore them, but in loose Palestinian peasant style rather than tight-pinned hair-hiding Islamic style, known as *hijab*. Ewa and Caoimhe, their experience and language skills making them more sensitive to nuances, tended to wear them more than we did. Jenny, living with Fida's family in the conservative Rafah area, wore one, Islamic style, always, except for actions where the Israeli army needed to see internationals were present. In the regions, Eva and I tied our hair up in headscarves sometimes, and sometimes we didn't; our devout friends in Jabalia never seemed to feel in the least bothered either way. In Gaza City we and Natalie (herself Lebanese) never wore them, along with several local women we knew.

One evening after the war, I was at the *shisha* cafe across from Al Quds hospital, visiting with the male volunteers I knew, plus local woman Amy, who taught *dubke* dance to Red Crescent volunteers including her own daughter. She wore no scarf, and gave me a brief lecture on the lack of necessity for the one my hair was tied up in. I offered a few excuses – like being culturally respectful, and downplaying my presence at a cafe where there were rarely other women – but then gave in and offered the real reason: 'My hair needs washing, alright!'

DECEMBER 23

Three images from today:

The first: looking out of the ISM apartment to see the Free Gaza boat *Dignity* speeding towards the port, finally bringing Vik back after his kidnap by Israel, and two Qatari delegates from the Eid charity delivering an aid cargo. I think the locals must have been up all night sewing maroon and white Qatari flags.

The second: standing in farmland only a few hours after a resistance fighter had been killed by a rocket there, surrounded by sheep, goats, and farming folk, who with indefatigable Palestinian hospitality offered us the only thing they had on hand – freshly pulled carrots. While we munched and took notes about the incident, the Israeli unmanned 'drone' plane buzzed ominously overhead. It's always up there, so you simply have to go about your day beneath it. Until it starts firing rockets. Then you have to run.

The third: standing beside the hospital bed of unconscious 9 year old, Sari, a kid who had been playing on his bike just a few hours ago. I ached to scoop him up and free him from the numerous tubes and monitors intruding into his small body, even though it was they that were keeping him alive. 'This is what the Israeli rockets do to our babies,' said the doctor, reaching with a cloth to catch the blood continually flowing from Sari's nose.

We'd heard reports of two children struck by one of these drone rockets as they played, so we'd visited Kamal Adwan hospital and spoken to Dr Ali Abd, the surgeon who initially treated them, and Dr Wissam Hiazi. They explained that one child had shrapnel wounds to face, neck, arms, abdomen and legs, but both children had brain injuries. One child required brain matter to be returned to the cavity. After cleaning and bandaging the wounds and treating the children for shock, the doctors sent them to Al Shifa hospital which has neurosurgery facilities.

At Al Shifa hospital we met the uncle of one of the boys, who confirmed that there had been no Palestinian missiles fired from the 'factory area' where the boys were attacked. Sari Al Sama'na, 9, and his friend Safi Al Sama'na, 8, were playing on their bikes at 2.45pm when a drone fired a rocket between them.

The doctor caring for Sari explained he had lost a great deal of blood, and only in about three days' time would it be clearer whether death, paralysis, or recovery with brain damage or psychological trauma awaited him. Safi was still in emergency surgery, his brain injury even more severe. The doctor estimated that 30 per cent of his rocket- or missile-injured patients were children, and another 30 per cent women or elderly people.

While in the hospital we visited three more patients. Mohmin Qraqe, 21, is a journalist who was working on farmland on December 7 in the Jabalia area, when at 3.30pm a rocket fell just two metres away. He has lost both his legs from the very top of his thighs. He told us that his father had been killed in the First Intifada when he was 7 days old, in 1987, and his 20 year old brother was killed by a drone rocket four years ago while attending a youth camp. He was living at home to be with his mother, as his older brothers were all married. He says he heard no Palestinian shooting before he was attacked.

Mohammad Abd El Nabi, a journalist for Al Quds Radio, went to Beit Hanoun last Tuesday to record a report on an Apache helicopter attack on two women that same day. He was flagging down a taxi when a rocket blast fractured his arm, and he sustained injuries to his head and leg. He was taken to hospital in a civilian car as the ambulances were already on calls. This is the second time he has been injured.

Zohair Washaha, 48, has a fractured leg and nerve damage after a ground to ground missile blast at 7am this morning while he worked on farmland near Al Wafa hospital. He heard no Palestinian shooting in the area prior to the attack. Zohair is the only breadwinner in a family of eleven, three of whom are at university.

DECEMBER 25

Things are definitely a lot worse than when I left in September. Rocket attacks and resulting injuries have increased this month, as the end-of-six-month-sort-of-truce date came and went last week. Talks are happening with Egypt's mediation, but everyone is getting more and more anxious. On a wild and stormy Christmas Eve I was reading the following:

> The Israeli foreign minister has indicated that an Israeli military operation in Gaza might be close at hand, as cross-border violence escalates between the two sides. Speaking on Wednesday to supporters of her political party, Kadima, Tzipi Livni said: 'Our desire for peace does not replace our responsibility to act when necessary, and now it is necessary…' News agency APTN reported that Israeli security officials, speaking on condition of anonymity, said that a large-scale military campaign against Gazan fighters had already been approved but delayed because of difficult winter weather conditions.[5]

Collective punishment is never 'necessary'.

I wanted to sit down and write a Christmassy email today, about us all ending up in the local Catholic church last night, and our sailor friend Mahfouz's little girls proudly making a Christmas tree especially for us despite their being Muslim.

Instead I am dashing round the flat in the dark looking for camera chargers and things, about to go out and join the other ISMers in Rafah, responding to a rumour that Israel has threatened to 'collapse' (bomb? destroy with an incursion?) the Rafah tunnel network that keeps everyone fed, if it's not closed down in 24 hours, 'because' weapons come that way also. First we heard the threat was true, then we heard it was false, now it's moved onto 'maybe'. Bear in mind that Israel has only been letting twelve basic commodities through the border (that's when they're in the mood, which they haven't been much lately) and the UN says it's not enough to prevent starvation. Unless the siege ends, Gaza folks need these tunnels.

In the shops, there are plenty of vegetables that can be grown here, loads of strawberries which Gaza produces and would love to export, and there's still chocolate (it's a luxury of course) but in the last days, people have been queuing for hours for bread. Our flat ran out of gas a few days ago, and there's no sign of any more (no more boiled eggs for me, and *no tea*). Mahfouz's wife Ridda still managed to cook us a wonderful meal last night, but I don't underestimate the achievement, or the expense.

And of course, another 24 hours may pass with only a handful of rockets, a handful of deaths, which somehow passes for 'normal' here. My visit to Rafah might simply involve lots of visits and friendliness. And everyone will go on, waiting tensely for the next rumour – or the tanks – whichever comes first.

DECEMBER 26

So it seems that what happened yesterday is, Israel dropped fliers in Rafah, saying that if the tunnels weren't closed in 48 hours, they would destroy them. I'm back in Gaza City today to sort out various things, but on call to return to Rafah if this threat is followed through tonight or tomorrow. Today Israel let some things through the borders they control; I guessed this was setting up a scenario to say 'we let supplies through the borders, therefore Gaza doesn't need the tunnels', but my friend Moh saw it as a sign they weren't going to attack after all. Who knows?

I was sent back to Gaza this morning with fresh-baked bread for me and Vik and Eva, having watched Fida's mother and sisters make it in a traditional earth stove in the corner of their garden, as Palestinian women have done since time immemorial. 'We are in paradise,' said Fida, 'because we still have flour and gas.' Back in the city however, Vik was cooking pasta when his electricity came on – but his happiness only lasted a moment – because immediately afterwards, his gas ran out.

Fida's family have a house in a quiet area of Rafah – well, I say quiet – yesterday someone was killed by rockets nearby. It is surrounded by olive trees, vegetables, and loofahs growing on a vine (I always thought they came from the sea…). But it took the family a long time to make their way to this comfortable home after their borderland house was demolished by Israeli bulldozers, and Fida remembers when they all slept in a makeshift structure of a few square feet.

Anyway, back to our Christmas Eve. About 700 Christians from Gaza applied to go to Bethlehem, which is really just round the corner and everyone used to go for Christmas. 150 of them were given permission. So some of them would have been with us in the Catholic church in the old town of Gaza City. We weren't paying the date much attention, but then we heard of the service, and as soon as we walked through the church gate, there it was – Christmas.

Father Emmanuel Musallam wore some rather fancy shiny silver robes, and someone's baby had a sequined Santa hat to match. The three solemn little altar girls in ankle socks kept jingling their bells accidentally at the wrong times, and then having to be nudged at the right times. But then, we ourselves were hard put to figure out when we were meant to be standing up and sitting down.

The church was painted with Bible scenes in bright spring colours, labelled in ornate Arabic script. Glittering chandeliers hung from the sky-blue ceiling, contrasting surprisingly with the fluorescent strip lights on the matching walls. I spent some of the service being intrigued by what I thought was a big mural of the young Jesus with God the Father, pleased to find that God was so friendly-looking, but then I realised that it was Joseph, and Mary was on the other side hidden by a pillar.

Father Emmanuel played keyboard, but also sang plainchant in the most beautifully pitched, rich bass voice. Some of Mother Teresa's nuns were present, and her picture hung beside the Christmas tree. Below it, brown paper mountains hosted a variety of animals, what appeared to be trays of wheatgrass ready for juicing, and another small Mary and Joseph on their travels, with Joseph in a blue polyprop head-dress, proving once again the versatility of polypropylene rope, an item of faith among my former fellow road protesters.

Moh scribbled a simultaneous translation of the sermon for us... 'He is reminding them of their legitimate right to Jerusalem, to Bethlehem, to dignity, life, celebration.' And to any who had given up: 'The Christian who doesn't shout "no" to death and "yes" to life is not Christian. We must reject the injustice, the crimes oppressing us. This isn't about politics, this is about life.'

After church, we hurried to the Kabaritis' seaside house, to find that the little girls had set us up a Christmas tree. I have spent a past Christmas in Bethlehem, where the population is actually half Christian, but I thought that Muslim folks here in Gaza might not pay much attention. In fact, everyone is wishing us Merry Christmas and many are taking the opportunity to be festive. I guess folks gravitate towards any bright spark in these difficult days.

Finally, Eva just sent the following to the ISM website:

According to Khalid from Shifa hospital, Safi Al Sama'na has improved and has been moved from the ICU. Unexpectedly, he is conscious and oriented. Sari still lies in critical condition, on a life-support ventilator. Since publication of the December 20 shelling incident which seriously injured the two young boys, there have been conflicting reports on the source of the rocket – some have said it could have been a malfunctioning Gaza-made one. The source of the rocket as stated in the original report was given by two different doctors, as well as one family member.

While we were visiting Zohair in the hospital, someone said to him 'ya 'tiik il-afiya'. I'd learnt this expression in Beddawi camp in Lebanon, finding it easy to remember because it sounded like it had both 'tickle' and 'laugh' in it. People said it to anyone working, and I understood it to mean, 'keep up the good work'. After the hospital visit I said to Eva – 'Zohair was lying on his back with his leg suspended. He wasn't doing much of anything. What does *ya 'tiik il-afiya* actually mean?'

'Well,' she said, 'for a long time, I thought it meant "can I get out of the taxi here please?", because it's what people say when they want the driver to pull over.' We pondered this for while, and ended up figuring out that it must be a bit like the poetic Irish expression 'more power to your elbow', and be applicable to anyone putting effort into anything, including a difficult recovery. In the context of taxis, we decided it must translate (very efficiently) as 'Well done on your sterling work as a taxi driver in bringing me so efficiently to the place I want to get out – which, incidentally, happens to be right here.'

3
DECEMBER 27, 2008–JANUARY 4, 2009

The Sky Falls In

DECEMBER 27

I was at home beside the small Gaza port, eating a bread and jam breakfast, when the rockets began to fall at about 11am. Six or seven deafening explosions occurred not far from my building, which rocked from the impact, smoke and dust filling the air. This occurred just as the children were on the streets walking back from school, and when I went out onto the stairs a terrified 5 year old girl ran sobbing into my arms.

Vik later ascertained that the F16 jets had targeted the port police station, and also the 'President's Palace' nearby, killing about 20. At the time of the attacks, Eva was on Omar Muktar street where a police station had just been hit, and witnessed a last rocket hit the street 150 metres away where crowds had already gathered to try to extract the dead bodies. The street was littered with rubble, making it difficult for ambulances and cars to get near enough to take bodies away.

Al Shifa hospital in Gaza City is full of dazed, wounded people – and pieces of what were people. Eva stood outside the hospital, watching as car after car, as well as the small number of functional ambulances, rushed in, bringing the dead and severely injured, and now she is inside documenting with one of our team.

We also have a team documenting in Rafah in the south. We are hearing that over 100 are dead and over 200 wounded. Several of the police stations that were targeted were having training days, but the dead and wounded include civilians and children.

Eva has just heard that the mother of her friend, who gave her a beautiful traditional Palestinian dress, is dead in the attacks on Jabalia. And Moh told us that the Israeli military has announced that these strikes are only the beginning. These rockets are killing civilians, *not* solely targeting Hamas. The many policemen killed and injured just now are government employees – they deal with traffic offences, petty crime. Women and children are dead. The police station nearest us was right by a school.

DECEMBER 28

In the basement, the family began the night at their allotted sleeping spaces, but as the hours pass draw closer together until women and children are huddled together in a pile of blankets. The women have slept little, and look exhausted. There are five or six children under the age of 5, tousled hair and solemn faces. The oldest boy's face is pinched and distorted with anxiety. Explosions are sporadic; sometimes far off, sometimes close.

The drone of Israeli aircraft is constant. Fragments of news come by phone. Attack beside Al Shifa hospital; windows explode onto patients. Security and Protection Forces attacked. Al Aqsa TV offices attacked. Plastic factory attacked. The number of dead increases in small leaps.

Multiple reports that Israel is phoning people at home, telling them 'any house with weapons in it is a target and should be evacuated'. And the usual calls about 'return Gilad Shalit and everything will be just fine', as if any of these civilians know the first thing about his detention. If they answer 'we don't have any weapons in our house and we don't have Gilad Shalit either', will Israel just bomb the neighbours instead?

Palestinian and Israeli Prisoners

In June 2006, Israeli soldier Gilad Shalit, then aged 19, was captured by Hamas activists who had crossed the border into Israel. Since then he has been held captive, probably by Hamas.

Soon after, a statement from the Izz ad-Din al-Qassam Brigades, the Popular Resistance Committees (which includes members of Fatah, Islamic Jihad and Hamas), and a previously unknown group calling itself the Army of Islam offered to release Shalit if all Palestinian women prisoners and those under 18 were returned.

In summer 2009, a number of rumours emerged that Shalit was on the verge of being transferred to the Egyptian authorities after talks with Hamas but this never happened. In October 2009, a minute-long video of Shalit was released, looking 'thin but healthy' and holding a newspaper dated September 14.

The international media's treatment of Shalit's captivity has been contrasted with its lack of interest in the fate of nearly 8,000 Palestinians held against non-criminal allegations in Israeli prisons, including over 500 in 'administrative detention,' i.e. without any form of trial, over 100 women and over 200 minors. Many were jailed by military tribunals which do not follow international norms for fair trials. As at December 2008, six of those held under administrative detention were minors.

Israeli human rights NGO B'Tselem has particularly criticised the fact that all but one of the prisons used by Israel to detain Palestinians are inside Israel. Travel restrictions imposed since the beginning of the Second Intifada mean that very few Palestinians are granted permits to enter Israel, effectively cutting prisoners off from their families for the entirety of their sentences.

Human rights organisations and prisoner support groups allege that Palestinian prisoners in Israeli jails are subject to terrible ordeals including torture, overcrowding, sleep deprivation, denial of family contact and education, sexual harassment and solitary confinement.

References: CNN, 'Militants issue Israel hostage demands', July 1, 2006; *Ha'aretz*, 'Shalit transfer to Egypt is imminent', June 26, 2009; B'Tselem, '2008 Annual Report on Human Rights in the Occupied Territories'; B'Tselem, 'Barred from Contact: Violation of the Right to Visit Palestinians Held in Israeli Prisons', 2006; MIFTAH, briefing on Palestinian prisoners, 2005.

4.30am: deafening bang, flare of fire, windows break, the children shriek and each mother grabs her child. One of the young women was on the basement stairs, and she is carried in, sallow with shock and fear, to be cradled by one of the older women. I give her honey sweets, since the more desirable sugary tea appears beyond anyone's capacity to produce right now – perhaps there is nothing even to heat water with. We cautiously venture up the stairs; an unfeasibly large crater has appeared outside, courtesy of an F16. Olive trees are the only casualties, but this is a little field in amongst residential houses. There is nothing here that even Israel could begin to describe as a legitimate target.

5.30am: 'Where is grandma?' asks one of the little girls. Grandma represents treats and other good things, which would be pretty welcome right now. 'Grandma is in paradise,' is the weary answer. Yesterday morning no-one could find any bread in the nearby shops. So Sara had set off, determined to track some down to feed her grandchildren. The first sweep of attacks at 11am caught her in the street, killing her by shrapnel, and leaving her body covered in dust. Eva knew her because she was a friend of Sara's daughters-in-law Nermeen and Fatima (the latter feeds her small boy under the blankets beside me) and their husbands, Sara's sons. So we came to pay our respects, but fearing an Israeli army occupation of their house, as happened to them during the March incursion, the family asked us to stay. Sara's teenage daughter is helping care for the children, but when things are quiet her face drifts into blankness.

In that first sweep of attacks, in about ten minutes, 205 people were killed and about 750 injured. Most government buildings and other social infrastructure were destroyed. Eighty Israeli planes and helicopters were involved in the attack and over 100 bombs were dropped.[1] So before this night began, the hospitals and mortuaries were full, the staff overwhelmed, the medical supplies exhausted.

Later...

8.00pm: Explosions begin again near to us and Al Shifa hospital here in Gaza City...

The Rafah team are continuing to document events there; we have heard that desperate Palestinians are trying to break through the border to Egypt, and it has been confirmed that Egyptian forces are shooting at them. We have also heard that twelve lorries of aid came through into Gaza. Fida was speculating that Palestinians would try to take the border wall down again.

Israeli tanks are massing at Rafah and also at Beit Hanoun. Ewa and Moh have gone to our contacts in Beit Hanoun for the night. On the way, they witnessed rocket attacks in Jabalia, on a car painting workshop and a metal factory.

Eva, Vik, Alberto and I are hoping to arrange to travel in pairs with two Ramattan news agency vans to whatever happens, to document events, but also shifting into high visibility as internationals if there is an incursion – being with families or riding with ambulances. If there is an incursion into Jabalia (no tanks there yet but it was an entry point in March) then Eva and I will try to reach the family we stayed with last night.

My phone is ringing constantly for press interviews. Maybe the world is finally beginning to listen. I hope so, because we are very much afraid things are going to get worse.

DECEMBER 29

Last night my group went to Al Awda hospital in order to be in the Jabalia region in case of incursion. One of the targets bombed by Apache helicopters was a mosque near us; the nextdoor shop and house were also destroyed, the rubble collapsing on the six daughters of the Balisha family.

I watched live footage as they tried to extract the single traumatised little girl who survived. The others were dead. We visited the site this morning, catching a ride back to Gaza City with a driver whose eyes were full of tears.

In Gaza I went to see the Kabariti family in the port area, who hosted us for Christmas Eve. They confirmed the entire Gaza coast was shelled all night from about 1am, with the shells apparently coming from Israeli ships too far out at sea to be visible. We could see this happening from the top of Al Awda hospital, counting 14 shells in a row at one point to the little port where the *Dignity* docks. Any boats linked to the Palestinian government were bombed, as well as several which weren't, including that belonging to human rights defender Dr Eyad Sarraj. When the extinguisher boat tried to put out resulting fires, it was bombed. The port offices were bombed.

The Kabariti family, whose six children range from 4 to 18 years old, had spent a frightened night and appeared exhausted. As they talked to me this morning, another missile hit the port across the road. I had not seen the family since the strikes began on Saturday; I spoke to their oldest son and daughter who described being at Karmel high school when rockets hit the building in the initial strikes. Habeeb said he had stayed outside the gate for a last five minutes' studying for his exam, thus avoiding injury when this happened. Now he doesn't know if the exams will even happen.

The children told me their 11 year old cousin had to carry an injured kindergarten child to the hospital when Al Wahda school was hit at the same time. The children's mother is worried about her parents; they live above a money exchange and the rumour is these will be targeted next; this has happened twice before in past Israeli attacks. They told me that in another area of Gaza a medical supplies storage building was bombed and the petrol station next door to it exploded.

Ewa and Moh visited the Islamic University which had six rockets dropped on it by F16s at around midnight. The five-storey Women's Building (in which I had attended some midwifery degree classes) and the Science and Engineering Laboratories are now mostly rubble. The damage extends to the neighbouring Al Azhar University.

These are only some of the multiple hits that occurred, just the ones I have been made aware of in a hectic day.

Tonight we are going to the same regional locations as last night. We have several arrangements to ride with ambulances visibly in case of incursion.

DECEMBER 30/31

Last night was a hectic scramble to get to our Jabalia house soon after dark; the further into the night, the greater the danger. On Sunday night, other commitments delayed us, and then over the phone the family said any car on the road late would for sure be hit and they couldn't bear any more loss, even new friends like us. So we arrived at about 6pm yesterday evening, and Fatima told us they hadn't spent more than brief moments up from the basement that day, since heavy bombing had begun at 5am.

The night was manageable; an Apache helicopter seemed perched above the house for a lot of it, but at least that meant it was firing rockets away from us. Nearer to morning we had some hours of it being the other way round, the explosions being pretty close. During the night, the Islamic University was bombed for a second time, and the port continued to receive attacks.

In the morning we went to document some of the attacks of the preceding 48 hours about which Fatima had told us. Fairly soon after we'd left, we heard the 'whoosh' of a rocket (gives you long enough to worry but not long enough to get away), heard the impact and saw smoke rise, from the direction of the house we'd just left. Eva phoned Fatima and found that the rocket had fallen beside the one from Saturday night; everyone was alright, but upset and scared.

Continuing along the road, we saw the destroyed yellow truck in which seven or eight members of the Sanur family were killed at 4pm Monday afternoon, as they went to pick up metal.

We continued on to the bombed-out shell of a washing machine shop and a carpentry workshop. The rockets had destroyed some of the home furnishings shop next door too, as well as blown holes in at least three neighbouring houses. The Abdul Hakim Eid and Eid Said Eid families' children of 4 months, 4 and 6 were injured in the attack. In the Akram Al Kanwa's family of ten children, seven were injured; two remain in hospital. An acrid aroma was in the air from the resulting chemical fire which had taken 13 hours to put out.

We were then taken to a chicken farm, which was simply ground underneath a building, open to the outside, with sawdust laid down, quite a nice place for chickens under normal circumstances. But either from shock or a physical effect of a nearby explosion three days ago, 11,000 were dead. The remaining 1,000 wandered about among the bodies, which the farmer was raking up and putting into bags. Vegans look away – that's 11,000 less dinners for Gaza families, not even counting the lost eggs.

Jameel Abdullah, with his sons Faisal and Abdullah, aged 5 and 2, showed us the huge crater in a field next to their house from Sunday's attack, which probably by design had destroyed a drinking water pipe. We heard of three teenagers struck by a rocket at between 11 and 12 in the morning; the 14 year old from the Abu Khater family was killed, and 13 year old Majd Migbel and 19 year old Mohammed Abu Nabi lost limbs.

While we were listening to this, Ewa called from Beit Hanoun hospital. She, Alberto and Moh had witnessed the arrival of 10 year old Ismail, Lamma, 4, and Haya, 12, from the Hamadan family, bombed that morning as they put out the rubbish. Alberto filmed as the doctors tried, and failed, to get Haya breathing again. Lamma died later in the hospital, and Ismail survives, barely. Ewa was told that Haya was a *hafiz* of the Koran – she knew all of it off by heart, every word.

3.1   Alberto films as Ismail, Lamma and Haya are taken to the hospital. Haya (on the cart) was dead on arrival, Lamma died shortly afterwards, and Ismail (in rescuer's arms) the next day.

Mohammed Rujailah

Initially at least, the Spanish newspaper that accepted stills of the children (taken by Palestinian Moh) said they could only accept for publication a picture of someone dead if their eyes were closed. We talked a little about that this evening. Eva and I think, if a child's parents have to see her dead without 'sanitisation', then so should we all.

At Al Shifa hospital today head nurse Khalid gave us a crash course in first aid – in case we are riding in ambulances or involved in an attack and we need to stick cannulas into people, or into each other. As is traditional in such training, the biggest and strongest person – Vik – turned the faintest.

Khalid told us they now have 29 ventilators in the ICU. Normally they have twelve, but as the worst-injured people are being transferred here, they've grabbed more from other hospitals, and now there are only a handful anywhere else. So basically only about 35 patients in all of Gaza (1.5 million people) can be kept alive if they arrive needing ventilators. Even if someone only needs a day for her body to regain its basic functions, if there is no ventilator free, that is a day too much.

Khalid also told us that yesterday someone purporting to be from the 'Israeli Defence Forces' rang Al Shifa to say it must be evacuated as it would be bombed. Al Shifa refused out of principle and of necessity. There is nowhere else to evacuate patients to. Sometimes these are hoaxes. Sometimes not – the same threat by phone was made in the last days to people in their homes. They left. The homes were bombed.

Today has felt quite strained. I find by the afternoon, I greatly need to upload all the experiences and information I have gathered from evening, night, and morning onto my webpage. Otherwise there is no room in my head. But today, Marna House's 'Cafe with Net' didn't have net. And then I got to Delice Cafe, whose windows are all broken, and for an hour the phone didn't stop ringing long enough for me to even order food, let alone begin to type. And then when I got back there after first aid training, Delice (perhaps because it is usually occupied by a small handful of journalists) had its own bomb threat and we all got unceremoniously chucked out. Our other two internet cafes have already given up and closed.

This morning also, we heard that the *Dignity* – which was attempting an emergency run to Gaza – had been confronted by eleven Israeli gunships in international waters at 5am, 90 miles from Gaza and 45 miles off the coast of Israel. The gunboats told them they had to go back to Cyprus or Israel would stop them because 'they were carrying terrorists'. Those actually on the boat included Cynthia McKinney, a former US congresswoman and Green Party presidential candidate,

Dr Elena Theoharous, a surgeon and Cypriot MP, and Karl Penhaul, a CNN correspondent.

The *Dignity* folks replied they would not be stopping, and gunboats responded by ramming them three times.

This damaged the engine and breached the hull, causing the *Dignity* to start taking on water, so they put out an SOS call. Cyprus Free Gaza folks lost contact with them for a while, but later heard that they had fixed the engine to some extent and were limping towards Lebanon, welcomed by the authorities there. We now understand they have arrived safely. And bless them, they plan to find a new boat and try again asap.

Israel's comedy explanation for ramming the Free Gaza boat:

According to the Israeli Foreign Ministry, the captain of the aid boat carrying several journalists attempted to evade one of the Israeli missile ships. The Israeli ship stopped, but a collision could not be avoided.[2]

Um, run that by us again!

Right now, we are working in a seafront apartment, which appears to be the only place in all of Gaza tonight with both electricity and internet.

8.40pm as I type. Whistling of shell from the sea. Phone check – Prime Minister's office totally destroyed.

Five minutes ago. Another whistle. I duck this time (yeah, like that would help).

Just now; much closer – we hear the crack of the explosion. After some thought, we move out of the front room.

Anyway, I'll – *hmm, that one shook the building.*

In the interviews I've been doing, they keep asking me – so are you in a safe place right now? And I answer – right now, there is no such place in the whole of Gaza.

NEW YEAR'S DAY 2009

Last night Eva and I accompanied Khalid on the dark walk from Al Shifa hospital (his day shift) to Al Quds hospital (his night shift); he didn't expect to find a taxi to take us, as our destination was past lots of government buildings which had received many strikes. His route attempted to avoid the main targets.

'Let's go this way to avoid the Jawazat police station,' Khalid said.

'Where exactly was that?' Eva asked.

'Oh well then, let's go past it so you can see it,' he offered, Arabic hospitality to guests immediately outweighing any concerns of being underneath a second-strike missile. The Jawazat was one of the police academies that were having a training day, and between 45 and 50 young men were killed there in the first ten minutes of attacks.

At Al Quds hospital we met the Red Crescent ambulance folks, who have set up a makeshift operations room in a hospital office. Round the corner, they have a perfectly good Operations Centre, but it has an unexploded missile in it, so it is hard to tell how much longer it will remain perfectly good for. I get the impression that whoever might once have been the person to ring to defuse unexploded missiles probably is no longer alive after all the police station strikes. The other buildings that are part of the Red Crescent hospital complex are a Social and Cultural Centre, also funded by them, with an emergency and obstetrics department in the basement. The middle building has various pieces falling off. And all of this is a result of there being – last week, anyway – another police station, just a little further along in this line of buildings. Now it is reduced to rubble.

Saleh from the hospital told us about some of the supermarket customers across the road, killed as a result of the first day of strikes. 'A 17 year old patient of ours had his father visiting. The father had gone to the supermarket to buy some things for his son. He was killed. And there were children just let out from the neighbouring school. I found two girls, aged 9 and 12. One died quickly of abdominal injuries. The other was missing part of her head and shoulder when I found her.'

We are here to arrange for internationals to ride with Red Crescent ambulances (along with government ambulances and any other medical vehicles) throughout Gaza. Everyone we have spoken to first reinforces how dangerous this work is, and then gratefully accepts, in the hope that an international presence will protect the medical workers who the Geneva Convention ought to be robust enough to protect, but isn't. Two have died in the previous few days. Israel seems to be following a two-strike pattern – bombing a particular location, then hitting again during the attempt to rescue the trapped and injured.

After the details are sorted out, our new colleagues insist it is too dangerous to walk or drive back to our home, and provide us with tea, dinner, and a comfortable room to ourselves for the night. Its windows are broken, but so are pretty much all the windows in Gaza City, including our apartment building. And there are lots of blankets. Eva and I feel very taken care of, as we always do in Palestine. What feels like extremely close rocket strikes begin just after I get into bed, and the door is pushed out of its frame by the impact. The staff come to see if I am frightened, and to karate kick the door back into place.

But the same thing happens again shortly after, and throughout the night. In the early hours, Vik texts from the seaside apartment to say the rockets are coming very close, just 100 metres off, and he is worried about the Kabaritis. But we all survive into the first morning of 2009. The nearby Ministry of Justice and the Ministry of Education are not so lucky, and what was left of the Ministry of the Interior also received more strikes. Rafah was hard hit. Injuries have exceeded 2,000 now, and deaths 400.

Today I went again to visit the Kabaritis, who spent last night together in their central room, with the most possible layers of walls around them, not sleeping. They are increasingly exhausted. Ridda tells me that as she feared, the money exchange over which her parents live was attacked, but they are ok. With binoculars, from their front window onto the sea, we can just see the Israeli ships that have been firing shells in our direction for several days now. Later, at the Ramattan offices where we give a press conference about riding with the ambulances, I take advantage of the broken window on the ninth floor to watch the smoke rise near the shore after each of the strange multiple booms of the shells from the sea. From here I can see six Israeli ships clearly. It is a beautiful, sunny day.

JANUARY 2

I've been asked to send some messages to a couple of the worldwide rallies on Saturday (yay!), and decided that I would much prefer to let Palestinians speak for themselves, especially some of the 50 per cent of Gaza's population who are under 18 years old (if you only remember one statistic, that's the one you want). I slept last night in a sea of blankets with the Kabariti girls, and thank goodness, there were fewer attacks on the port than the night before and they could get a little sleep. They have provided me with very neatly written messages to the world, which I promised would be on my blog before their bedtime. So here they are –

From Suzanne, 15 (in English):

The life in Gaza is very difficult. Actually we can't describe everything. We can't sleep, we can't go to school and study. We feel a lot of feelings, sometimes we feel afraid and worry because the planes and the ships, they hit 24 hours. Sometimes we feel bored because there is no electricity during the day, and in the night, it is coming just four hours and when it comes we are watching the news on TV. And we see kids and women who are injured and dead. So we live in the siege and war.

From Fatma, 13 (in English):

It was the hardest week in our life. In the first day we were in school, having the final exam of the first term, then the explosions started, many students were killed and injured, and the others surely lost a relative or a neighbour. There is no electricity, no food, no bread. What can we do – it's the Israelis! All the people in the world celebrated the new year, we also celebrate but in a different way.

From Sara, 11 (in Arabic, translated by Habeeb, 18):

Gaza is living in a siege, like a big jail: no water, no electric power. People feel afraid, don't sleep at night, and every day more people are killed. Until now, more than 400 are killed and more than 2,000 injured. And students had their final first term exams, so Israel hit the Ministry of Education, and a lot of ministries. Every day people are asking when will it end, and they are waiting for more activist ships like the *Dignity*.

From Darween, 8 (in English):

I am a Palestinian kid. I won't leave my country, so I will have lots of advantages, because I won't leave my country, and I hear a sound of rockets, so I won't leave my country.

Mariam is 4. Her siblings asked her, 'What do you feel when you hear the rockets?' And she said, 'I feel afraid!'

People have asked me if I am frightened. What I am frightened by is the enormity of these events, at how few international eyes are here to witness them, and that it is hard to imagine how it will end. In the last handful of days, I have given about 30 interviews by phone, and a couple on camera, to a world outside which my friends tell me is slowly waking up to this disaster. Yet about 400 foreigners took up Israel's offer of an exit route through Erez today, and we wonder what Israel has planned next that it doesn't want outsiders here to witness.

I am so glad to be here, to be a small sign to Gaza folks that people do care about them. And my fabulous friends are sending supportive messages, not only to me but to Palestinians, who cluster round to look at them, and translate them to each other, sometimes in tones of astonishment; and to smile at the footage of demonstrations and vigils. I told a local friend today that Israelis will be demonstrating against their government's actions on Saturday, and she could hardly comprehend it. I look forward to sharing the pictures of this and all the other rallies about to happen, with her and everyone.

Beneath the rockets is a strange place to be, that's for sure. So far, most of my little ISM group seems to have the same calm response to this crazy scenario, and that is helpful. During the day we catch taxis (largely to save time as well as for safety) if they are going where we need to go. If we are going to dangerous areas, or at night when the taxis vanish, we tend to walk. We prefer to avoid paying someone to take us somewhere dangerous anyway.

Walking through this ghostly city at night is easier with a colleague for company and consultation. Everyone, including the taxi drivers, take circuitous routes designed to avoid as much as possible both places that have been bombed (as repeat strikes are not the less common for being pointless) or places that might be bombed.

This process is becoming increasingly intricate. Last night, Eva and I began the route to the hospital as we had done the night before, choosing what had been the safe-ish route then. We didn't realise (until we found it looming above us) that this route, yesterday watched over by the elegant and massively solid Palestinian Legislative Council, now included its enormous remains. I am awed by how much power it must have taken to destroy it. We stumbled swiftly over the rubble, rockets occasionally lighting the sky, in time for us to cover our ears.

I think there might actually be some registered taxis in Gaza, but I never bothered figuring out how to spot them. In normal times, you need never wait more than minutes before almost anyone driving will pull over to take you where you need to go.

Half the time, it will be someone subsidising his own trip's expensive fuel by collecting a carload made up of anyone waiting on his route; often, it will be someone who simply wants to help a foreigner. If the driver is lacking change he will improvise with sweets. Very often, whichever category he falls into, he will refuse any payment at all. I began to carry chocolate bars to pop onto the front seat when it had been made clear that money would offend.

Several days into the aerial bombardment, five of us decided we needed to get to Jabalia. No sensible person was driving there, on the assumption that any car, possibly any light, would have a bomb dropped on it. But a Ramattan press friend conjured up the one taxi driver in Gaza who thought a drive under these circumstances sounded like fun.

As we left the city centre and found ourselves on empty roads in pitch blackness, it suddenly sunk in that we were very, very vulnerable, and possibly very, very stupid, and I for one found myself wanting to get where we were going very, very quickly. Our driver, on the other hand, wanted to ask Alberto (in the front seat) all about Spain, and what he thought about life in general, and he slowed down more and more so he could concentrate on the conversation.

Squashed in the back, we were overwhelmed by hysteria-tinged laughter when he stopped altogether to try and obtain cigarettes from somewhere in the blackness. We all filed him on our mobiles under 'crazy driver' and saw a lot more of him over the next days of very sparse transport.

About 14 mosques have been bombed since Saturday. Early on, after covering the destruction of the mosque that had also killed the Balisha girls, Vik and I had to pass a beautiful one in Jabalia. An old man explained we had come the wrong way, and said we had to go back past what he called the 'mosquito'. We did, edgily. I heard yesterday it no longer exists.

There used to be a lovely house overlooking the sea on Charles de Gaulle street, surrounded by one of the few gardens with lush green grass. In August when I was first here, I would peer in through the railings as I passed. I discovered yesterday it is rubble, just a white staircase left climbing to nowhere. I am told it was the governor's mansion from the time of Egypt's rule here in the 1950s, used mostly since the 1960s to host dignitaries.

Not someone's home though. The Al Quds doctors were telling us that most of last night's targets in Rafah were homes.

I was thinking about rubble, and how it all looks the same, though the buildings it once constituted all looked different. And how tiring and sad it must be to clear it by hand, when you maybe haven't eaten or slept enough. Especially if it is your personal rubble.

I haven't slept a night at home since the strikes began, but I do manage the occasional visit for a wash. And to eat jam with a spoon since it is the sole foodstuff at my place.

At least one more emergency medical worker was injured today. Ahmed Eid, 25, was attempting to rescue people in the just-bombed house of the Babish family, in the Sheikh Radwan area east of Gaza City at about 4pm, when Israeli planes took the opportunity for a second strike. Six or seven civilians were injured and Ahmed required stitches to his head. There are unconfirmed reports of injuries to another medical worker. Three children were killed by rocket attack in Khan Younis. At 1.30 this afternoon, Dr Hasan Khalef from Al Shifa told us that in the last 24 hours, 20 children have been killed and 112 wounded, and eight women killed and 135 wounded. Ismail, the third child of the Hamadan family, died yesterday of his injuries.

To be absolutely honest, if this goes on for weeks, I don't think all of my ISM group will make it out alive. But are our lives worth any more than those of the people of Gaza?

JANUARY 2/3

Last night (January 2) Eva rode with the Palestinian Red Crescent in Jabalia, where attacks have continued to be very heavy, and was witness to the collection of three martyred folks – one the 24 year old caretaker of the American School, whose body was in a terrible state as a result of the school being bombed during the night.

Our Jabalia friends, Fatima's family, had further near misses during the night and were very distressed, so Eva went to see them this morning. She found that Israel had dropped leaflets in the area announcing that everyone must leave their houses because they will be destroyed. So Fatima's family, with all their little ones, have today left behind what must now seem like the comparative safety of their basement. But Eva met the neighbours, who have ten children, and are not leaving – because they simply have nowhere to go. Also Sara's husband, Fatima's father-in-law, is not leaving the neighbourhood, though he won't stay in the empty house. I guess he's just had enough, and perhaps only wants to join his wife in paradise.

Our local colleague Moh told us of a teenager from his youth group who died yesterday. A 16 year old Christian girl, Christine Wade'a al Turk, died of a heart attack brought on by a severe asthma attack, resulting from the stress of the ongoing strikes.

Bombing across the road from me at the port this morning destroyed further boats, filling the sky with thick black smoke. One wonders what the point is. Vik and I will be with Jabalia's Red Crescent Service tonight.

Shortly after I got this far with this draft, we had to go to Ramattan for a press conference stating that though 400 internationals left yesterday, many of us are remaining to stand beside our Palestinian friends. And to state our belief that Israel wants no outside witnesses to its next actions, and perhaps no possibility of being called to account for the deaths of any inconvenient Westerners. At about 5pm the rumour reached us that the army's ground incursion was about to begin, and we dropped everything else to run to the Red Crescent in Jabalia…

JANUARY 3/4

5.30pm: Ramattan media office. Shelling has noticeably increased in the last hours. Rumours increase that the Israeli Occupation Force

3.2   The broken-windowed Ramattan press office offered us wi-fi and a view of smoke rising over Gaza. Eva and I spent hours on our laptops writing reports while Vik paced the floor giving telephone interviews.

Sharyn Lock

will begin the land incursion tonight. We hear that a mosque in Beit Lahia has been attacked during prayer time, resulting in 50 injured and maybe ten dead. We decide to head immediately to Jabalia's Red Crescent ambulance operations centre, which is a walk from Fatima's house which the family has left.

6.00pm: When we arrive, there is chaos and anxiety, as the ambulance workers have just finished dealing with the mosque injuries which included children. Explosions are constant and nearby. We understand that these are coming from tanks shelling the area from the other side of the border, a new development.

7.00pm: Some semblance of calm has returned to the Operations Centre but not to its surroundings. A white phosphorus rocket lands in the field beside the centre. The explosions continue through the whole night without pause, rocking the building. We can see many people leaving the area on foot. We hear a water tank is destroyed.

7.30pm: Ambulances called out. We are unable to pass a huge crater in the road into which a car has already nosedived. Taking the long way round, we collect a man in traditional dress, in his sixties, from what seems to be his family farm. He is bleeding from the face and very frightened. On the way to Kamal Adwan hospital a particularly close explosion rocks the van. I mustn't have jumped enough, because the driver mimes 'did you hear that?' to me. I am beginning to realise Palestinians are fond of rhetorical questions, such as 'how do you find Gaza at the moment?'

8.00pm: We collect a man in his thirties from a family house in a main street. He is continually bleeding from the face near his eye and also has wounds to his hand and upper and lower legs. He has made makeshift bandages for himself. We take him to Al Awda hospital. On the way back we pick up a woman and her daughter who are in danger having gone to collect water.

8.20pm: Bread and tea at the Centre. Ambulances called out.

8.40pm: Medic worries 'we are taking too long; ten minutes'. However at our dangerous and darkened destination no-one arrives in response to the ambulance loudspeaker, the electricity lines are down, and smoke fills the air. The ambulances retreat, describing it as a no-go area. Immediately beside it, a farming family of about ten emerge from the smoke, looking bewildered. Some of the children are crying, everyone is holding tight to each others' hands. One woman is pregnant. The medics shout at them to leave the area, then decide to evacuate them in the ambulances. We drop them in the nearest town, to go god knows where.

8.55pm: We hear the Israeli army has crossed the border – in Rafah, in Gaza centre near Bureij camp, and here in Jabalia. We hear Israel has told the Red Cross (the communication medium) that people must evacuate to a distance of 1km in this area. I glimpse a teapot and tea but we are called out again.

9.10pm: We collect two women. I am not sure what the issue is, although the younger woman appears pregnant. We deliver them to Al Awda hospital where we are given tea. Hassan, one of the medics, tells me about his three children and his wife, who is very worried about him.

9.30pm: Back to the Centre for short period of quiet (except for the noise). Our driver has decided he likes me because my beret reminds him of Che Guevara. He is driving with his arm in plaster.

10.00pm: Ambulances called out. A family of about twelve was round the fire outside their house, having no other way to cook or get warm. They were hit by a rocket and all are injured. Many ambulances converge at Kamal Adwan to transfer them to Al Shifa in Gaza City which has more resources. The wounded are pushed into one ambulance after another. We have a young man, perhaps a teenager, whose breathing is being done for him by a medic with a handheld pump. I can't help but wonder if one of the 29 ventilators is free right now. But our driver says afterwards that he probably won't survive the night.

10.55pm: We leave Al Shifa to head back to the Jabalia Centre. There is coffee. Moh makes a coffee sandwich, which is just weird. There is a pause. Hassan asks about my book, *Nature Cure*; I explain it is about an ecologist's route out of depression. 'People get depressed in the West?' he asks in surprise. Understanding how implausible that must sound right now, I say that many people get caught up in a life that mainly holds work and buying stuff; and without some sort of meaning – religion, or the dream of your land being free, or creating a sustainable society, or something like that – people can get very lost.

'Actually Israel is trying to force us into a meaningless life like this,' he says. 'Like, sometimes I feel that all that really matters to me right now is a kilo of gas. I built a stove for my family and I feel like I did something amazing.' The discussion becomes animated as all the medics join in, but it's in Arabic. We have a quiet patch – again, despite the noise.

1.00am: This is a call to a woman in labour. Vik has a similar call. What a night to give birth. The stress is bringing on labour early for many women. Hassan says he should have documents for her to hand in at Al Awda, but they've not been allowed through from the West Bank for some time.

At this point I lose track of the time for a while and also get a couple of hours sleep. When I wake I find that Alberto has come back from a grim call. The ambulances were called to the Beit Lahia/Salatin area, outside the local school, to assist the Atar family. However the IOF[3] forced them to turn back by dropping a bomb in front of the ambulances and shooting in front of them, so they were not able to access the wounded.

However, as they turned back, a donkey cart pulled in front of Alberto's ambulance. On it were an older man and woman, probably the parents of the three teenage boys on the cart. One of the teenagers was attempting to shield the other two with a blanket. One of these two had a serious head wound and his eye was detached. The other had an open chest wound, and his arm was partially detached. Despite this he was conscious and shouting. Alberto could see his lungs, one appeared punctured, and the clearly disturbed mother was patting his wounds. Back at the Jabalia Centre, Alberto described in quiet horror how he had assisted the medics lifting this boy off the cart, and in doing so, found his hand had slipped inside the boy's body.

6.00am: My ambulance goes to three women, waiting in the dark street. They are young and quietly weeping. One carries a boy of about 4, wrapped in a blanket. His head flops back and his eyes are half open. I find myself hoping maybe he has just fainted from fright. Eventually I understand, perhaps from the weight of grief on their faces, that he is dead. We deliver them to the hospital.

6.30am: Several of the ambulances leave to try again to reach the Atar family. Mine only gets a short way before rubble bursts a tyre.

This appears to happen nightly. While the medics try to fix it, we see a rocket strike very close to the Ambulance Centre. By the time we get back from getting spare tyres, we have been told not to return to the Centre as the shooting is now right near it.

8.15am: We return to evacuate the Centre as the army is now very close. People on the streets are running away. We move our base to someone's shop in a Jabalia main street. No more tea kettle or generator.

9.30am: Three ambulances attempt to reach wounded. We wait to have access co-ordinated with Israel by the Red Cross. Israel refuses.

9.45am: Israel broadcasts the message all over Gaza: 'For your own safety, leave your homes immediately and head towards the city centre.' Many people have been on the streets this past night, carrying children and bundles, and now the number increases. But there are also many people simply waiting at home, without any belief in a safe place. A rocket hits near us while the ambulances are all off. The injured man is pushed into a car, which rushes off.

10.50am: We collect an old women from a farming area. She is very distressed and has a bullet wound to her upper shoulder. The medic inserts a cannula into her arm despite the bumpy road.

11.30am: We go straight from the hospital to another call. As with many of our calls, locals line the way, pointing the ambulance to the correct turn. A house has just been bombed. Neighbours are frantically dragging out the wounded and the medics cram four people into our ambulance, which is meant for one.

The stretcher place is taken by the dead body, covered in dust, of a man in his thirties. His abdomen is ruptured and damaged organs visible. His legs look as if they no longer contain bones and are twisted implausibly. One foot detaches as he is put in the ambulance. Another man, maybe older, looks to have internal injuries and might also have injured legs, but the chaos is such that I can't clearly identify his injuries, or those of the man in his sixties, who is shoved into the remaining space. He is in shock, sweat covering his grey face. I helplessly stroke his cheek, wondering if he is about to stop breathing. Halfway through

3.3   Ahmed Abu Foul, Jabalia Red Crescent. The evacuation of Jabalia's Red Crescent offices occurred on the morning of January 4, due to its being targeted by the Israeli army. The medics, including recently married Ahmed, then worked out of several different makeshift locations throughout the attacks.

Eva Bartlett

the journey, his eyes focus slightly. I hope not enough to realise he is crushed against a corpse. The injured boy of about 3 is held in the front seat by his father.

At Kamal Adwan hospital, a wail of grief goes up from all waiting there at this scene of disaster. They haul out the living, and we are left with the dead man. We move the ambulance away from the delivery area. Our medic strokes the man's face. 'Actually, he was my friend,' he tells me. 'His name was Bilal.'

We are told that since last night 47 people are dead, twelve of them children, and more than 130 injured. These numbers are increasing as more people are found and more die from their injuries.

3.55pm: Just after I posted the above, Eva heard that one of the medics on the Jabalia team – Arafa – was shot and killed.

4.55pm: Unconfirmed report, another medic has been killed in Al Sheikh Rhajleen.

JANUARY 4/5

6.00pm: To Al Awda hospital, run by the Union of Health Work Committees. It normally has a 50 bed capacity but has been stretched to 75. Eva and Moh interview Ala'a (the medic from Jabalia Red Crescent who was severely injured when Arafa was killed yesterday) in his hospital bed, in between his moans of pain. The story goes as follows:

It was about 8.30 Saturday morning in Jabalia. Five teenagers found themselves under shell attack and tried to get away. Three escaped. One, Tha'er, 19, had his foot blown off. His friend Ali, also 19, tried to pick him up and carry him to safety, but was shot in the head and killed. It took 75–90 minutes before an ambulance could reach them. Medic Arafa, 35, and Ala'a, 22, carried Tha'er to the ambulance, and then went back for Ali's body. As they closed the van door, they were targeted with flechette shells, whose metal darts and shrapnel shred your insides.

Ala'a says, 'I felt nothing – just that I was flying in the air and then falling.' Including the medics, about ten civilians were injured. Other ambulances evacuated all. Arafa, who was married with five children, had a severe chest wound with most of one lung gone and he only survived two hours. Ali's head was blown off. Ala'a is now in hospital with severe shrapnel wounds all over, especially chest and legs, and is likely to spend at least his near future in a wheelchair. Tha'er survived with lacerations to back and body from the flechettes.

Arafa was a teacher for the UN, gave medic training, and volunteered as a medic after being one professionally earlier.

7.00pm: We arrange to sleep in shifts at Al Awda hospital. Vik and I crash. Eva, Alberto and Moh hitch a ride with the first Red Crescent ambulance that turns up, out to Kamal Adwan hospital, the Red Crescent's second new base since evacuating their centre. The base is a few blankets in a corridor, but there is tea sometimes.

11.00pm: Eva comes back to sleep, Vik and I ride with Omar's ambulance to Kamal Adwan. Omar has a scarf wrapped round his knee, he was shot there some years ago and has pain in cold weather. I talk Alberto and Moh into going back to rest, but fail to convince Ewa. She seems to have sworn off sleep altogether, which I scold her about. The night turns out to be quiet. Unfortunately, I soon understand this is because (a) a lot of Jabalia people have run away, and (b) Israel is not letting the ambulances collect most of the wounded that do call for help.

2.00pm: We collect a woman in labour. Back at the hospital, I chat to Osama, who is a nurse but volunteers at the Al-Assyria Centre that the Union of Health Work Committees runs. Also to Mohammed, in a hospital bed. He is 23, six months married, and made the mistake of standing next to the Jabalia mosque that was bombed two days ago. He is now recovering from abdominal surgery. Ewa and I are being phoned hourly by the BBC to contribute to news bulletins, 'live from Gaza', yet I notice they've only called us to do this in the middle of the UK night.

5.00am: We hear that there has been a threat to bomb Al Wafa hospital, which is a rehabilitation centre.

7.15am: We collect a man seriously injured by rocket explosion from a house in Sikha Street, Jabalia; watching his face I doubt he has more than minutes to live, but he is still alive when we reach the hospital.

9.00am: We collect a woman whose home has just been shelled, she is having a panic attack and I am not clear on her injuries. Back at the hospital people are loudly grieving for two recent dead. These may be the nearly dead man my ambulance collected and another I saw arrive, both horribly mangled by rockets and the now-familiar grey colour.

9.30am: We hear that Beit Hanoun is almost completely occupied by the Israeli army, as is the nearby small town, Zahra, which commands the north/south road. The north (us) and the south (Fida, Stelios, and Jenny in Rafah) may now be cut off from each other. We check in by phone, making contingency plans.

10.00am: Moh's sister calls to tell him his village of Khoza'a is being shelled; the farmland in the centre which is surrounded by housing. 'There's nothing there, just people's homes,' he tells us. He says there are now Israeli tanks in the 'Atatra area of Beit Lahia. This is 1km inside the border, and 2km away from us at Jabalia. He says tank invasions used to take main roads, but he expects this time they will do what they did in February: bring in bulldozers and go directly through the houses.

He tells us that today Palestinian phones are receiving recorded messages from the army, saying 'To the innocent civilians: our war is not with you, but with Hamas. If they don't stop launching rockets, you are all going to be in danger.' This can only be psychological game-playing. Everything I have seen suggests the Israeli army doesn't even understand the concept of 'innocent civilians'.

11.50am: Call to near Gaza beach, turns out to be a mistake. Instead we pick up a family with two little children who are evacuating, sat on the side of the road, worn out from carrying bags. We passed Beit

Lahia UNRWA school earlier, it is filling up with refugee families. Like the Lebanese army's 2007 attacks on Nahr Al Bared refugee camp, all over again. Will there be no end to UNRWA schools full of frightened people?

The Samouni family

The fate of the Samouni family became one of the most horrifying stories of Operation Cast Lead. The facts slowly emerged as follows: on Saturday January 3, 2009, approximately 100 members of the Samouni family and their neighbours took shelter in a house in the Zaytoun area of Gaza City. Many of them had been sent to this house specifically by Israeli soldiers entering and attacking nearby homes.

On the Monday, some of the men went out to try to gather firewood. Two were immediately killed by a shell, and two others wounded. Minutes later, the house itself was shelled, killing dozens. Some fled; others stayed behind.

On Wednesday 7th, the Red Cross was permitted to take the survivors from the house, having been denied access to the area since the initial attack. At least 48 people had been killed; some of them had died of their wounds while waiting for the ambulances. Four children were said to have spent two days clinging to their mothers' bodies.

After the survivors were evacuated, the IDF prevented access to the area until after January 18 and bulldozed the house on top of the remaining bodies, ensuring that medical evaluations could not be carried out.

According to Amnesty International, 'The ICRC [International Committee of the Red Cross] said that the Israeli soldiers stationed nearby must have known of the people in the houses but that the wounded died as they waited for medical care due to the slow negotiations for access.' Newspaper reports also described how neighbouring houses had their walls daubed with graffiti including: 'Arabs need 2 die', 'Die you all', '1 is down, 999,999 to go', and scrawled on an image of a gravestone the words: 'Arabs 1948–2009'.

References: Amnesty International, 'The conflict in Gaza: A briefing on applicable law, investigations, and accountability', January 2009; *Guardian*, January 19, 2009; *Telegraph*, January 9, 2009; Amnesty International, 'Operation Cast Lead: 22 days of death and destruction', July 2009.

Medic Naim draws my attention to one more extremely crowded bread queue, and then we discover a young teenage boy in the queue has collapsed from exhaustion; the medics treat him to the extent they can.

4.00pm: Fida calls to say they've heard Al Awda hospital has been shelled. I ring Ewa. She says a structure immediately beside it received two shells; one person was injured, the man who lent her his jacket last night. He has shrapnel to the head and she says he isn't looking too good. Alberto apparently caught the shelling on his camera. We wonder if we should head back there to be with Jabalia Red Crescent instead of Gaza City RC.

Latest: There have been two separate reports about Israeli attacks on funeral tents. We are trying to confirm deaths and injuries for one. The second of the funerals attacked was medic Arafa's yesterday afternoon; five killed and about 40 injured.

We have also had reports that in the Zaytoun area two days ago, Israeli soldiers rounded up an extended family into one house, possibly as many as 100. Then this morning at 11am Israeli forces shelled the house. We have heard the number of deaths as between seven and 20. One was a 7 year old boy whose father was interviewed on TV while holding his body. We are trying to find out further details. It is getting very hard to keep up with this insanity.

The Jabalia Red Crescent's base is now a makeshift desk in a section of the carpark underneath Al Awda hospital, outdoors. It's cold. We ask the dispatch co-ordinator sat at the desk how many of the emergency calls Israel is not letting them go to. These are in areas where co-ordination must be made with the invading forces via the Red Cross to enter. He says they are not being allowed to attend to about 80 per cent of the calls from the north, covering the Beit Lahia, Beit Hanoun, and Jabalia area.

Shall I repeat that? *80 per cent*. Eight out of ten people calling for help are being prevented from receiving it.

'Co-ordination' and medical access

The Fourth Geneva Convention states that 'Medical personnel of all categories shall be allowed to carry out their duties.'

Over the last decade the Israeli military has, instead of allowing ambulances and paramedics to reach wounded civilians as a right, instituted a system whereby the Red Cross acts as a 'coordination mechanism' for the 'entrance of important vehicles into areas of Israeli control. These vehicles [include] ambulances of the Ministry of Health or the Palestine Red Crescent Society.'

This co-ordination involves both sides using the same types of satellite maps to determine exact positions. According to Physicians for Human Rights (PHR):

> In case of need, a request to access a controlled area is first directed to the ICRC, which informs the Israeli military (COGAT – Coordinator of Government Activities in the Territories). This unit contacts the ground troops in the area, from where authorization or the refusal of authorization is then transmitted in the same way backwards. In the beginning of the existence of this mechanism it took about one hour to get authorization or refusal. In October 2008 it took about five hours. During the recent attacks the time increased to sometimes more than one day. It took four days to reach the attacked area of Al Zaytoun.

The Gaza Red Cross also told PHR that 'there was never a clear definition of areas where "co-ordination" would be required' and as a result there were many cases during Operation Cast Lead when ambulances were turned back for not having IDF authorisation. PHR stated that in total 160 requests for authorisation were received during Cast Lead and that the ICRC will analyse these, but the results will only be discussed with the Israeli authorities and not be made public. PHR also stated that 16 Red Crescent and 13 Gaza Ministry of Health ambulances were damaged during the invasion.

Reference: Physicians for Human Rights, 'Independent fact-finding mission into violations of human rights in the Gaza Strip during the period 27.12.2008–18.01.2009', April 2009.

4

JANUARY 5–JANUARY 16, 2009

No Safe Place

JANUARY 5

8.00pm: I am due at Al Quds hospital for a Red Crescent shift at 8pm, but as I am finishing writing with the seaside apartment's generatored electricity, the strangest noise arrives from the sea. It is a whooshing sound like a rocket coming very close. Vik and I look at each other over our laptops, look at the seaside window – he pulls his fisherman's cap lower and leans away from the window, I put my borrowed jacket over my head so I can't see what happens. But instead of finishing with an explosion, the sound decreases again into the distance.

It is then repeated several times, and I realise what we are hearing is not rockets, but F16 planes – very loud and incredibly fast. I set off to walk the half hour, unlit route to Al Quds hospital, but am only half way up the hill when more planes speed over, and deafening explosions start between me and the hospital. I completely lose my nerve, stopping still under a tree and texting Eva that I can't do this walk by myself. The planes have freaked her out as well. I walk quickly back to the apartment, and try to work out what to do. Vik suggests I walk the other direction, to Al Shifa hospital, and catch an ambulance shuttling to Al Quds.

What is it with these planes? This little strip of land doesn't even have a proper army! The term 'overkill' has never had more meaning. It takes me some time to summon up the courage to set off again. Luckily the evil planes have gone.

10.45pm: I am still at Al Shifa, having been waylaid by a Press TV reporter wanting to do an interview, but I've got into an ambulance ready to head off. Just as it is about to leave, rockets fall either side of the hospital and we retreat hurriedly back under the entrance shelter.

By the time we get to Al Quds the atmosphere is hectic. They have just received three men who were in a car outside a house when it was bombed. I am not clear if one is dying or already dead. We rush another of them to Al Shifa for neurosurgery. Then we are sent off at high speed to emergency calls, through a darkened city full of smoke. Double strikes by Israeli planes happen so often now that the ambulance workers' stress levels are very high; the medics are doing everything at top speed and yelling as they do it. Rubble covers the streets from strikes just minutes ago. The familiar smell of exploded concrete fills the air, the same smell of the grey lifeless men we have collected in the last days. I think of it as the smell of rockets, and of death.

We peer into the darkness for someone watching for us; we spot a young boy who runs back around the corner. He returns with his family, 25 of them, mostly terrified young children. One boy is hopping. The medics run to grab them, shouting what must be the equivalent of 'Move, we've got to get out of here!' Everyone is shoved into ambulances; a whimpering girl of about 6 is posted through the half open window into my arms. Instinctively I fold her into my arms so her face is hidden, so for a little while she can see nothing frightening and hear as little as possible. We tear back to the hospital, offloading them into comparative shelter, racing back to collect a father with his daughter of about 8 in his arms, a head trauma case.

Later, I go to see the family of 25, gathered in a room where they have been given blankets and food. There don't appear to be any serious injuries, though when I hear more that seems a miracle. I ask two articulate and beautiful English-speaking teenage girls, Ra'fat and Sa'ida, what their story is. They explain half the family is their aunt and her children, who came to their house because their own was destroyed. Ra'fat says – 'In the last three nights, we were hit 13 times the first night, three times the next, and tonight ten times. The third floor was gone, then the second floor, we were just left in the first floor, now there is almost nothing.' They translate the aunt's words to me – 'What is the solution for us? What?' The girls add, 'We had no solution from Fatah. No solution from Hamas. We just want peace! Just peace!'

'Where will you go?' I ask them.

'We don't know,' they say. 'We have some other family but they left their house too because Israel threatened to bomb it. We don't know.'

I hear from Eva that she was borrowing internet time in the Sharuch office block tonight, which houses Russia TV, Fox, and other press offices, when it was struck seven times one after the other. She got safely to the ground from the tenth floor, with everyone else, but she says she feared the whole place was going to collapse.

There is confused news through the night of more attacks on mosques and homes throughout Gaza. After the hectic earlier hours, the middle part of the shift is filled by collecting five women going into labour; by the fifth call volunteer medic Musa thinks his dispatcher is joking. I am pleased to be able to smile at our patients. Then Musa tells me about a 17 year old woman who went into labour yesterday. Her sister-in-law's 1 year old had been killed in her arms, the bullet continuing on to wound the mother. Her father-in-law is dead, but his body has not been able to be collected. They have not told her that her husband is also dead.

4.00am: Behind the two reception desks opposite each other are two families sitting on plastic chairs put in a circle. They are silent. A medic explains that the residential building behind us here at Al Quds has had a bomb threat. These families have evacuated to us here. Others remain in the building.

6.00am: I speak to Ewa in Jabalia on the office phone. The Red Crescent ambulances have again relocated their base, since there was concern that Kamal Adwan hospital – a government hospital – might be a target. So Ewa, Moh and Alberto have done the night shift from the new base of Al Awda hospital. Ewa says that at about 5am, four ambulances went to collect wounded from a house attack. They returned to get further wounded, again in a convoy of four, and the Israeli army shelled the house for a second time as soon as they arrived. The medics outside the vans were injured by flying rubble. Ewa was inside the van.

Musa tells me there was an attack on an UNRWA school, by Apache he thinks, which killed three UNRWA volunteers helping with the refugees. He is asked to collect the body parts, as they are near the bathrooms which is distressing for people. But the Red Crescent boss says his is the only ambulance on standby so he must wait till others return first.

5.00pm: We just heard in the last hour that the Al Fakhoura UNRWA school was shelled, we think by tanks, and it is confirmed that 43 members of the same extended family were killed. The UNRWA schools are sheltering refugees whose homes Israel has already bombed or threatened to bomb. I cannot express the anger I am feeling right now.

Our group is holding together but we are feeling the increasing strain of not enough internet access, food, sleep or hope for an end to this insanity. The numbers of dead have exceeded 570 and the injured have exceeded 2,600.

Attacks on UN staff and facilities

The United Nations Relief and Works Agency (UNRWA) was established in the wake of the *Nakba* in 1948, when 700,000 Palestinians became refugees. In the last six decades, it has run the housing camps, schools, clinics and food aid operations which still support many Palestinian refugees – the largest refugee population in the world.

Despite its vital humanitarian role and its close co-ordination with the Israeli authorities, a number of attacks took place on UN facilities during Operation Cast Lead. Human Rights Watch, listed these:

▶

January 15, at least three white phosphorus shells struck the main UNRWA compound in the Rimal neighborhood of central Gaza City, wounding three and starting fires that gutted four buildings and destroyed more than US$3.7 million worth of medical supplies. According to UNRWA officials, they had been speaking with IDF officers throughout the morning as the shells landed progressively closer to the compound, asking them to halt fire.

About 700 civilians were sheltering in the UN compound at the time.

At another well-marked UN facility – a school in Beit Lahiya sheltering roughly 1,600 displaced persons – the IDF air-burst at least three white phosphorus shells on January 17, the day before the cessation of major hostilities. One discharged shell landed in a classroom, killing two brothers who were sleeping and severely injuring their mother and a cousin. The attack wounded another 12 people and set a classroom on fire... the UN had provided the IDF with the GPS coordinates of the school prior to military operations.

Prime Minister Ehud Olmert alleged to United Nations Secretary-General Ban Ki Moon, who was visiting Israel at the time, that Palestinian fighters were using the Rimal compound as a base for attacks. UNRWA's Gaza director John Ging 'denied that any Palestinian fighters had entered the compound, let alone fired from it'.

Amnesty International added that large quantities of food aid, including flour and cooking oil, had been destroyed by phosphorus fires in the Rimal compound. Amnesty also reported that

Israel not only failed to adequately supply the population of Gaza, it also deliberately blocked and otherwise impeded emergency relief and humanitarian assistance... On 8 January 2009...a UN aid convoy was attacked in the north of Gaza, killing one UN-contracted employee and injuring two others. The UN said that it had coordinated the convoy's movements in advance with Israeli officials.

References: Amnesty International, 'Operation Cast Lead: 22 days of death and destruction', July 2009; Human Rights Watch, 'Rain of fire: Israel's unlawful use of white phosphorus in Gaza', March 2009.

4.1   Medic Hassan at work in Jabalia during the early January attacks. Hassan was shot in the leg in Jabalia on January 7.
Mohammed Rujailah

JANUARY 7

The other day I described how I was working with Hassan and he was telling me he couldn't get home, and how worried his wife was about him. Today he was shot by an Israeli sniper.

Alberto just got back from the scene and he describes events as follows:

At 13:10 Jabalia Red Crescent got a call to Dawwar Zimmo, east of Jabalia refugee camp, very near where the Red Crescent centre was that we had to evacuate the first night of the land incursion. Two medics, including Hassan, a driver, plus Eva and I went.

People on the street directed us ahead, saying it was a *shaheed* civilian further up the street that we had been called to. We continued and located the body. The two medics got out and put the *shaheed* on the stretcher, but while covering the five or six metres to the van, 13 shots were fired in our direction. One hit the ambulance. One went all the way through Hassan's upper thigh. The medics had to leave both *shaheed* and stretcher to get into the van, and shooting continued as the ambulance pulled away. One of the medics speculated the sniper may actually have been firing from the Jabalia Red Crescent centre.

I have to go now to my ambulance shift…and Hassan is at Al Quds hospital, so I am really wanting to see him.

Attacks on medical personnel and facilities

According to Physicians for Human Rights, during Operation Cast Lead 'There is absolutely no doubt that the number of medical institutions, such as hospitals and mobile clinics were specifically targeted including a large number of ambulances…[and a] number of patients died as a result of the delay in transportation to a medical institution.'

According to Article 56 of the Fourth Geneva Convention: 'To the fullest extent of the means available to it, the Occupying Power has the duty of ensuring and maintaining, with the cooperation of national and local authorities, the medical and hospital establishments and services, public health and hygiene in the occupied territory… Medical personnel of all categories shall be allowed to carry out their duties.'

During Operation Cast Lead, however, this Article was contravened on many occasions, including:

- the attack on Al Quds hospital and Red Crescent compound using white phosphorus lumps, white phosphorus artillery shells and tank shells (see box on page 88);

▶

- the killing of three paramedics, Anas Fadhel Na'im, Yaser Kamal Shbeir and Raf'at Abd al-'Al, along with a 12 year old boy who was showing the paramedics the location of wounded men. They were struck by Hellfire missiles, marked as made in the USA and probably fired from an Apache helicopter. The IDF prevented their bodies from being collected until two days after the incident;
- the killing of volunteer paramedic Arafa Hani 'Abd al-Dayem (see January 4/5);
- the killing of Dr 'Issa 'Abd al-Rahim Saleh, a 32 year old doctor, on January 12 while he was attempting to rescue residents of a Jabalia apartment building which had been shelled. Dr Saleh was directly struck by a missile which decapitated him, caused shrapnel wounds to a paramedic helping to carry the stretcher, and killed their patient.

Amnesty International stated: 'The Israeli army media briefing of 22 April, in the section on "incidents involving shooting at medical facilities, buildings, vehicles, and crews", contends that "Hamas systematically used medical facilities, vehicles and uniforms as cover for terrorist operations", but provides no evidence for even one such case.' Amnesty said that it did not exclude the possibility of such abuses, but stressed that no evidence had been provided and that the burden of proof fell on the Israeli authorities.

References: Amnesty International, 'Operation Cast Lead: 22 days of death and destruction', July 2009; Physicians for Human Rights, 'Independent fact-finding mission into violations of human rights in the Gaza Strip during the period 27.12.2008–18.01.2009', April 2009.

JANUARY 6–7

Al Quds hospital, to which I have shifted my base from Jabalia, has a small Intensive Care Unit, watched over some of the time by head nurse Khalid. It is a sad kind of ICU; almost nobody will leave it. The incursion means many of the staff cannot physically get to their hospital jobs, so everywhere is short staffed. Al Quds have sent most of their surgeons to Al Shifa. So they've made Al Quds ICU into a place for what Khalid calls 'cold cases': head-trauma patients, victims of explosions, who are brain-dead, on ventilators, and not going to wake up. They need basic nursing care only, but still nurse M'an hasn't been able to go home since Saturday.

Tonight the ICU holds a boy of 14, a man and woman both 23, and a 30 year old doctor. The doctor was working in a mobile clinic in Surani, Shuja'iyya, when one of the initial Saturday 27th air strikes targeted a nearby police station. She won't recover. Sometimes when I hear stories like this, I think of things like all those years she studied medicine, all the exams she must have worked so hard for, all that time and effort.

Strangely, in the midst of these people slowly coming to an end, is one more patient, but he is recovering. I don't like to ask if they thought he wouldn't and that's why he's here. I originally saw him in Al Shifa, when he was unconscious and on one of the precious ventilators. On my first visit here a few days ago he still had a nasal tube inserted, now he is free of it and he can tell me about himself, in the educated English so many Palestinians have.

He is Mehat, aged 44, a teacher at an UNRWA preparatory school in Zaytoun. In the initial December 27 attack, he heard the strike on the police station nearby while he was out walking to get some fuel. But it was the F16 rocket attack on the Saraya building – the central office for police and security – that got him. He has had abdominal surgery, surgery for multiple fractures of his left thigh and foot, treatment for chest trauma, and he has shrapnel in his right leg. Two metres of his intestines have been removed; he is dependent on a colostomy bag, and it is too early to tell if this is permanent or not.

I am sure that a man with such a kind smile is not alone in the world, yet I have seen no visitors. He tells me his children are 9, 12, 15 and 16, plus a little afterthought aged 1 year 3 months. His parents live with the family also, neither are well. He has told his wife no-one should visit him because moving about is too dangerous.

I ask Khalid what happens when people are dependent on machinery and are not going to recover. He says the practice here is that life must be respected and must end of its own accord, even in these days of shortages. 'But,' he says, 'these patients don't stay long.' He tells me the 14 year old boy probably has no more than 24 hours left. And when I go to see Mehat again in the morning, the 23 year old woman's bed is empty.

I found out from Eva that Fatima, of our family from Jabalia, has a phone that can receive English texts, so I sent one to ask her how they all were now they have moved to stay with family outside Jabalia. She answered 'Hi, we are so glad to hear that u r ok. we r fine and we believe that we'll return back to our home, so nothing can stop our life to be continued. We love u and wish to see u soon.'

There is a collective strength to these people that dumbfounds me. Medical folks are quite a comic crew; one of them last night was carefully explaining to me that he didn't have to worry about dying of lung disease, because he was careful not to buy the brand of cigarettes that had the man dying of lung disease on it.

Later on, one of the Disaster Team had thrown us all out of their operations centre (normally the hospital director's office) and was washing the floor. It was chilly outside, so we were all lurking at the door wanting to come back in, but he was shouting the Arabic equivalent of 'Keep your filthy shoes off my nice clean floor!' Finally he installed the widest paramedic to function as a guard; he took up his position outside the door with folded arms, doing an excellent imitation of a nightclub bouncer. I suggested that when the Israelis got here (the tanks are shelling from 2km away now) we give him the task of keeping them out of the operations room. He assured us he was up to the job.

These people have lost friends and family in recent days, and face the risk of death each day. But Palestinians have a sort of collective unspoken agreement – everyone has to keep going for everyone else. I don't know what it does to their mental health; but then, I don't know what choice they have. The other day, our friend Halim asked Eva how she was doing; this was after the death of Arafa, the second of her friends to die in these strikes. She allowed him to see how upset she was. Later, he came to speak to us, tell us that we too needed to join in this unspoken agreement, almost the more because we came from outside. We should not give our friends here a chance to wonder if, from an outsider's viewpoint, the pain they must bear is in fact unbearable. He taught us a new word to say – 'ospr', or 'ospri' for a woman. It means – 'Be patient. Be strong.' Fida tells us that Rafah residents have been told to leave before they are bombed.

JANUARY 7–9

I covered another ambulance shift Wednesday night, working with two guys who might turn out to be my favourites. Musa is a light-hearted EMT driver with good English (very helpful for me) with the ambition to have a baby born in his ambulance, since so far he only knows the theory of the process. Ishaq is a dad of three, with a wife who he insists doesn't mind the idea of him having a second wife at some point. Musa is scathing about the concept of multiple wives.

Ishaq is happy for me to work as his assistant so that's pretty cool. I can actually be useful, especially when a medic is outnumbered; Wednesday night at one point we took on four injured people after a rocket blast near Palestine Square, all from the same home. A little boy with a head wound, two adult men, one with a head injury and the other with a leg wound. A young woman who hadn't any visible bleeding waited quietly until last, at which point we found that under her shirt, glass or shrapnel had entered deep beside her spine, so she got sent off for an X-ray on arrival to Al Shifa.

I'd heard that Hassan was here in Al Quds, but by the time I got here he'd been sent home, which was encouraging in terms of his wound, and certainly good for his family who hadn't seen him since the strikes

4.2   Inside a Jabalia ambulance rescuing an injured family on January 7. The young woman has shrapnel pieces beside her spine.

Sharyn Lock

began, I think. I've since glimpsed the footage Alberto took of his shooting, on Al Jazeera, so at least it's got that far, and I had reports of it being on New York TV.

Nurse Khalid's house in Khan Younis was bombed yesterday. Ishaq's was destroyed. So was Dr Basher's, and his nextdoor neighbour's. Dr Basher showed me the usual photos of rubble, his personal rubble. Three more homeless families taken in by relatives, whose houses may also be under threat. Is anyone's home going to be left standing?

Wednesday was the first day when there was a truce, from 1pm until 4pm. In that time, the Red Cross successfully negotiated for themselves and Red Crescent medics to enter Zaytoun, one of the places where

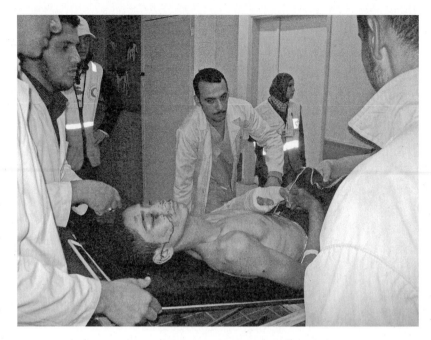

4.3   On January 7, the first Zaytoun evacuation was permitted. One of the injured children finally receives medical treatment in Al Quds after no rescue for several days.
Sharyn Lock

Israel has refused to allow emergency calls to be responded to. My medic friends described walking for about 4km in total, using donkey carts to bring out the few dead and injured they could; they only had time to reach four houses. At times they were shot at by the army despite the advance arrangements and the so-called truce.

The home of the Samouni family was one of the houses they reached. A medic told me that two days before, there had been a call from this house to the Red Crescent, saying that 25 women and children were there, with about five dead after shelling attacks. But on Wednesday when the house was reached, almost all were dead, survivors included one 11 year old boy with a leg injury. What shocked the medic I spoke to was that the majority appeared to have been killed by close-range shooting – it seemed an execution had taken place. I have not been able to find out further clear details on this, and in fact there are various confusing versions of this story, of seven families and 100 people in fact being in multiple houses together that were shelled. Ramattan journalists are going to interview a survivor in the hospital this afternoon so it may become clearer.

At other locations children without food or water were found beside dead parents. Some of the injured people brought out are here in the Al Quds hospital. I met baby Nour, tucked in a bed with her mother, and another woman with them whose child had been killed.

Following this I obtained permission to go on Thursday's Red Cross/Red Crescent evacuation back to Zaytoun again during the hours of ceasefire. My impression was they were glad of a second woman and another international. The team was made up of three Red Cross folks and about ten Red Crescent medics. A similar RC evacuation team elsewhere during ceasefire was fired upon, with one Red Cross worker injured. I am going again today, Friday, with the team from Al Quds.

We understand also that UN food deliveries were fired upon and one or two UN people were killed.

Last night for the first time I went back to my flat with the aim of getting a night's sleep, having not had more than two hours in a row in any 24 since this whole thing started. I wish I hadn't! Being away from Palestinian or international friends was hard, but being woken two hours into my longed-for sleep by the sound of shooting outside the house had me in complete confusion, since it wasn't coming from a hovering Apache.

As I'd finally seen Israeli tanks and soldiers today, and realised how close their lines are, my sleepy mind immediately decided they'd somehow reached the port area. The drones were also going crazy; normally they sound sinister but monotonous, now they sounded like a swarm of angry hornets, swooping about manically.

I started to think about what to grab for an escape back to my friends, but a little while later I got through to Vik on my mobile and he explained that the drones had started shooting, something us foreigners at least had no idea they could do. Rockets, yes, shooting, no. Last night, apparently for the first time, they began firing at anyone on the street. I shelved my escape plans, but then the hornets started swooping nearer and the rockets were rocking the building. So I jumped up, packed an emergency bag, got dressed in case I needed to leave in a hurry, moved my mattress the furthest I could from outside walls, and then miraculously managed to get back to sleep.

When I visited the Kabariti family yesterday, Mahfouz told me that the girls are asking him how much it hurts to get injured, and what happens if they die. They are seeing so many pictures of children like themselves wrapped in body bags. He has explained that God sends you into unconsciousness if you are hurt, so you don't feel the pain.

11.00am: I have just heard that the evacuation for today has been called off. Israel will not give permission for rescue. So this means more time to wait, for the people trapped in no-man's-land.

JANUARY 8

So, Thursday just past: the Red Cross co-ordinated evacuation into Zaytoun. Doctor Said would look good on a Red Cross poster – black sweater, shaved head, muscles enough to keep that Red Cross flag held above his head for the two hours we were behind army lines. You'd definitely invite him in for coffee to ask for his opinion on the state of the world.

His colleague has more of an accountant look about him, but his job is to keep us alive – he is armed with a walkie-talkie and is negotiating our path constantly with the army as we move. With May, a small, quick woman who is the Engineer for the Red Crescent, supervising all the vehicles etc, I carry a stretcher and water. About eight intrepid

Red Crescent paramedics and volunteers join us, wearing weighty bullet-proof vests, or not, depending on their preference for possible death or certain backache.

What startles me first of all is how close the IOF have come. I heard that they were 2km from the hospital but I guess I didn't quite absorb that – until we all jump in the ambulances to drive there, and then jump out again almost immediately. The Israeli Occupation Force is pretty much just round the corner. I haven't seen them in person since 2005. They ain't changed much.

Just as I occasionally forget that the planes in the sky are killing machines and assume for a moment they're just jetting folks off on climate-damaging holidays, my brain initially registers the sound of tanks as some sort of roadworks. Which they are in a way; they are unmaking the road. Salahedeen is the main north–south road and they're doing their best to make it impassable, with earth mounds and barriers and blockades made of bombed cars. Soldiers point guns at us from behind the earth mounds. Snipers cover us from occupied houses. We all hope Mr Walkie-Talkie is saying the right things.

He's very polite, and isn't in fact saying any of the things I would be saying if I was on the phone to the IOF right now. I guess that's why he has his job and I don't.

Walking past all these weapons is the point where anyone would reasonably get scared; for some reason (I discovered this on my first West Bank trip years ago) this doesn't happen to me. There's clearly a bit of wiring in my head connected wrong, and I think people who are scared and do stuff anyway are much braver than I am. Obviously I do get scared sometimes, but now (stupidly, one might say) just isn't one of them.

Maybe it's when I've got work to do. What I feel in walking this road with these good people is calm, and focused, and glad to be here. As my friends know to their sorrow, what I don't cope with is supermarkets and SUVs and plastic. Even more, I don't cope with the dissonance of trying to live in a Western society which pretends that this reality –

the reality of the road I am walking right now – does not exist. In the UK, in front of me is McDonalds, in my head are the tanks. It almost sends me crazy sometimes.

Out here the dissonance dissolves, and the relief is great. So yes, I acknowledge I have a personal agenda. We all do.

When I was a kid, I was very aware of war zones, but I always understood they happened in places different from my home. I would like to tell you about what I am seeing right now as I walk. I am seeing flowering vines. Bright curtains in windows. Chickens running about. This is your home, you know. This is the garden where your children play. This is your house with obscene holes blown in it, with Israeli snipers lurking in the shadows of its roof, with a dead resistance fighter sitting with his back to your wall.

'Red Cross! It's safe to come out! We can evacuate you!' everyone shouts up at the silent windows of the next house, the one after, the one after that. And eventually a lone elderly man appears from a house holding a white flag. And then a whole collection of faces behind a gate, hands reaching for our bottles of water. A dead teenage boy has been placed outside the gate. 'My son,' says a man simply to us, in English. We ask them to wait there and continue. After an hour and a half, we have collected about 80 people, at least half of them children and many elderly. For each turn off the path we make to shout at damaged houses, permission must be asked and granted. And yes, I did the Red Cross poster thing myself and carried a small child. Well, he only had little legs and we were in a hurry.

And strangely, the evacuation has its lighter moments; one of the paramedics has a tendency to attempt to catch any animal that passes him, failing however to get a hold on a chicken, duck, cow or goat. Actually the goats want to accompany us of their own accord anyway, viewing the whole thing as some sort of pleasure jaunt. Red Cross and Red Crescent alike are smoking heavily as they go, lighting each other's cigarettes.

In a straggly convoy we leave the silent houses and walk back towards army lines. 4pm is drawing near. In Gaza City, Israeli planes continue shelling during the supposed three-hour ceasefire, but here soldiers have watched us in an eerie silence, apart from the growl of tank engines.

When the children see the tanks, their faces twist, and they reach for their mothers' hands, some having to be forced to continue moving past them. Guns are trained on us. Now we can see the earth mounds we have to climb over, our vehicles on the other side. But! It's 4pm. Woe betide holding off the day's ceasefire end for another five minutes. Whoosh of a rocket, everyone tenses, it explodes just behind the building the ambulances are parked beside. Children stumble on rubble and begin to wail. Nearby gunfire begins.

And strangely, the point after we climb over the line and open our vehicles doors is when some of the adults begin to cry anxiously. Perhaps they think there won't be enough space for all – and we do have to shove people in, including into the ambulance carrying the three dead we stretchered out. 'Where is Yusef?' 'Where is Samir?' Parents lose sight of children and panic. But in the end we get them all in, and drive the unnervingly short distance back to Al Quds hospital, where people tumble out of the vans. And then there is a bright moment which I watch from a window above: families arriving and claiming their missing people.

I sit down to eat cold rice with the medics on duty, but before I can take a mouthful, get physically hauled up six flights of stairs to the kitchen by one of the medics who was on the evacuation, to find that being on today's team apparently merits very tasty scrambled eggs instead.

We hear that on another Red Cross evacuation, the army shot at and injured one of the Red Cross workers.

SOME MOMENTS OF JANUARY 9

...standing ten floors up in the Ramattan press building watching phosphorus shells falling on the eastern area of Gaza City, again and again, bright white smoke rising. This stuff can burn through to the bone; the doctors say they haven't seen anything like it. The thought of being underneath that does frighten me.

…discovering our final remaining internet/food cafe has been threatened with bombing and so has closed. We are *hoping* it's temporary. It is incredibly difficult to find ways to get information out now, since movement and electricity are so limited.

…while on ambulance shift, visiting Khalid of the lovely smile, who is tired and missing his family. Everyone in the hospital seems to have their family on the other side of the army blockade. The 14 year old boy in ICU is gone. In his place is a little one – Abed – almost a baby, his chest rising and falling with the ventilator's jerk. Enlarged pupils indicate the usual explosion-caused brain injury. Khalid realises his oxygen levels are low and swiftly begins to try to clear a blockage, asking me to hand him things. 'He will die,' says Khalid quietly, 'but he will *not* die of suffocation.' In the middle of this, Ishaq appears to hurry me to the ambulance; I tell him I can't come. Later I hear from him that the call turns out to be for three injured people from the same family after an attack on their house, their injuries involve missing limbs and holes in chests he has to try to seal. His face is sad and subdued – no access to his wife and three kids, his house demolished, and a damn hard job. I feel extremely bad I wasn't there to help, even just to share the weight of witnessing these terrible things.

…one of the medics telling me about a call the Red Crescent received yesterday, from a woman sobbing that she had no flour to make bread and could not feed her children. 'What could I do? All I had to offer anyone was an ambulance,' he said.

…coming home this morning to discover the fire station on the other side of the road is no more, and the road itself is a big crater. Glad I wasn't home for that.

JANUARY 10

3.00pm: Just posting this now from Ramattan. Their wireless internet is working today, thank goodness, and they don't mind us borrowing it. Moh stands at the window watching Israeli tanks shell buildings in the distance. As usual, smoke is rising in several locations. There is a press conference going on behind me about the fact that the government body managing the water here is now unable to guarantee waste water treatment or drinking water. I am hearing of more and more houses with no water at all. I suppose maybe next time I go to fill my water container there maybe nothing to fill it with. What happens then?

JANUARY 11

I am again at Ramattan watching these weird phosphorus bombs falling on the city.

From the Times Online, January 8, 2009:

> There were indications last night that Palestinian civilians have been injured by the bombs, which burn intensely. Hassan Khalass, a doctor at al-Shifa hospital in Gaza City, told The Times that he had been dealing with patients who he suspected had been burnt by white phosphorus. Muhammad Azayzeh, 28, an emergency medical technician in the city, said: 'The burns are very unusual. They don't look like burns we have normally seen. They are third-level burns that we can't seem to control.'
> Victims with embedded white phosphorus particles in their flesh have to have the affected areas flushed with water. Particles that cannot be removed with tweezers are covered with a saline-soaked dressing.
> Nafez Abu Shaban, the head of the burns unit at al-Shifa hospital, said: 'I am not familiar with phosphorus but many of the patients wounded in the past weeks have strange burns. They are very deep and not like burns we used to see.'

After the war, Italian documentary maker Manolo Luppichini interviewed one of the Al Shifa doctors, showing him an information flyer on the limited treatment possible for white phosphorus burns that had been provided to Israeli army medics. He became visibly upset. 'If only we'd had this in those first days, we could have saved some of our people… we didn't know what it was. We didn't know what to do.'

White phosphorus

White phosphorus ignites on contact with air and continues to burn at 816 °C unless starved of oxygen. In contact with skin it creates 'intense and persistent burns', down to the bone. Infection is common and the body absorbs the chemical, causing potentially fatal damage to the liver, kidneys and heart.

The use of phosphorus munitions is allowed under international law in certain circumstances – as an obscurant in open areas and against 'hardened military targets, such as bunkers'. However, air-bursting white phosphorus munitions over populated areas is forbidden because it cannot be used in 'a manner that adequately distinguishes between combatants and civilians'.

In March 2009, New York-based NGO Human Rights Watch published the results of investigations into allegations that Israeli forces had routinely air-burst white phosphorus in built-up areas in Gaza.

It stated: 'In Gaza, the IDF most frequently air-burst white phosphorus in 155mm artillery shells. Each air-burst spread 116 burning white phosphorus wedges in a radius extending up to 125 meters from the blast point.' It continued: 'the IDF repeatedly exploded white phosphorus munitions in the air over populated areas, killing and injuring civilians', and concluded that 'the unlawful use of white phosphorus was neither incidental nor accidental. It was repeated over time and in different locations… the IDF's repeated firing of air-burst white phosphorus shells…into densely populated areas was indiscriminate and indicates the commission of war crimes.'

According to HRW, targets on which the IDF used white phosphorus as an incendiary or against civilians include:

- homes and apartments in the Tel al Howa area on January 15;
- Al Quds hospital and Red Crescent administration buildings on January 15, forcing the evacuation of 50 patients and 500 sheltering neighbourhood residents (see page 96);

▶

- the main Gaza City centre UNRWA compound also, on January 15 (see page 101);
- an UNWRA school in Beit Lahia on 17 January, sheltering roughly 1,600 displaced persons.

HRW also determined that the IDF had air-burst white phosphorus on the edges of densely populated areas, possibly as an obscurant to mask military movements. Cases included Siyafa village near Beit Lahia (January 4) and Khoza'a village east of Khan Yunis (January 10 and 13), where 'substantial amounts of white phosphorus landed up to a few hundred meters inside residential areas, killing at least six civilians and wounding dozens'.

Reference: Human Rights Watch, 'Rain of fire: Israel's unlawful use of white phosphorus in Gaza', March 2009.

Moh has just been speaking to his sister. His family were receiving the phosphorus bombs all last night, in Khoza'a, east of Khan Younis. She said in their area there were 110 injuries from phosphorus. Today they fled their house and went to relatives. We called the Ministry of Health to ask if they have analysed the substances involved, but they said that they simply don't have the resources to do so and have to wait on outside confirmation.

Omar from the Jabalia medics appeared briefly yesterday at Al Quds, with an ambulance with bullet holes in. It had been shot at by an Israeli sniper on Friday between 1.30 and 2pm, and had to turn back without reaching its call-out. Five shots were fired, Omar said.

'Please take care of yourselves,' I said to him.

'If we die, it's ok,' he said. 'What will be left? I think no-one will help us.'

Last night I stayed near Al Quds but at a friend's house – they have no water. It was another night of heavy bombardment, with shells falling near the hospital, constant rockets, and Apache shooting. By the early hours of the morning there was shooting between the Israeli army and the Palestinian resistance very nearby, so that local people were coming to take refuge in the hospital. They left in the morning, but a steady stream of people, escaping their houses near the fighting, began to trickle past Al Quds.

The Israeli army refused the Red Cross permission for more evacuations from Zaytoun and other cut-off areas yesterday and today.

I went home to get my things so that if we in the hospital are cut off by the army, I'll have most of what I need. This could happen tonight, or this whole thing could drag on for days...

Khalid has managed to get to his family in Magazi camp, the first time he has seen them since their house was hit several times. He will try to get back as soon as possible since Al Quds ICU now has only one staff nurse running it. The little boy who he was caring for the other night when I posted died several hours later. His place has been filled by another explosion victim.

JANUARY 11–12

Writing from Room 101, the temporary ambulance dispatch room. During Monday there were some more evacuation attempts; it sounds like the one Ishaq was on got about 50 people out of three or four houses, but they think there are many left.

The one Musa was on didn't have any luck, the road was completely barricaded and they weren't allowed to leave their vehicles, so they shouted from where they were but weren't able to make contact with anyone, though they'd been getting emergency calls from the area. Musa came back startled by how close the army was. It's supposed to be his night off (between two 24 hour shifts) but he now doesn't want to leave the hospital, so he's just keeping on going.

Just now (a little after midnight, into Jan 13) two of the medics have made another co-ordination with Israel via the Red Cross to go into an occupied area to fetch a woman in labour. This *might* mean they're allowed to reach her and *might* mean they're not shot at while they try, but neither is guaranteed.

Today I went with Musa to eat at his family's house in Tel al Howa. His sister Rand gave me a hat and scarf she knitted herself (there seemed to be a general opinion I wasn't wearing enough warm clothes), his sister-in-law Wisal interpreted for me, and his mother not only made me herbal tea for my cough, involving *babounage* (chamomile), *maramiya* (sage), and *za'atar* (thyme, usually eaten on bread), but also filled a thermos for me to take away with me. (My dad sent me an anxious email the other day, urging me to get my cough checked. I've had coughs all my life when under stress as well he knows. I think this might be *slightly* displaced anxiety on his part.)

During my visit, Musa's cousin arrived. She and her husband had to leave their Shuja'iyya house after it was attacked with tank shells. She just went to look at it and was describing the fire damage to the family, the sight of which had clearly left her shocked and fragile. She is in her early twenties, if that, and as she sat quietly beside me, tears rolling down her cheeks, she held a cushion over her belly. She is pregnant.

I was talking to Duha today, who is also from Tel al Howa. She is a lively second-year medical student who volunteers with the Red Crescent Disaster Management team. Her family lived near a Ministry building there, which was attacked on December 30. Thirteen bombs in a row dropped on the building, breaking all the glass in the family's apartment and all the doors, even the mirrors and the cupboard doors. Her family had gone to the window to see what was happening, and the impact threw them all across the room. They have moved out to stay with relatives of their neighbours, who have taken in three families in total. Duha says they are lucky because they have the basement all to themselves.

I was showing Musa some photos of narrowboats today, including my friend Jack's boat in London with lots of plants and a wind generator and solar panel, plus a heron perched on top. 'Gaza doesn't have beautiful things,' he said thoughtfully. 'Just what we see in pictures or on television.'

I continue to give a crazy amount of interviews via the phone. I do best when asked to simply describe what I see around me. South Africa radio tends to want me to offer political analysis, when all I can honestly say is – 'I don't know what the hell Israel is trying to do.'

Ishaq tells me that about 25 Egyptian ambulances have arrived at Al Shifa hospital, delivering sorely needed medical resources, and – they hope – evacuating patients for whom Al Shifa doesn't have the facilities, out to Egypt.

Tonight in the hospital are three tiny new babies, triplets. They are sleeping soundly in their incubators, despite the tankfire that comes ever nearer. For them alone I don't want to leave the hospital now; we have heard some terrible rumours of what has been done to babies, apparently deliberately, and Alberto took some grim pictures. I was helping with the English translation of the testimony of the surviving Samouni family members whose house was bombed after they were put in it by the Israeli soldiers, and how one, a 20 year old mother, found her baby had been killed by shrapnel while she held him.

Someone was talking the other day about how the high birth rate amongst Palestinians really worries Zionist Israelis who greatly fear being outnumbered in this region. I made some comment about how families are losing not one but several children due to houses being bombed etc. And suddenly I thought – what if this attack is partly aimed at killing as many children as it can? Is it really possible someone in Israel has sat down and calculated how to do that? I just can't begin to think about this.

I am far more worried about being arrested than being killed. I would like to think I am not important enough for the army to bother with, and if they come into the hospital I can monitor and document and challenge their behaviour if need be ('cos a load of guys with guns are really going to listen to me, right?). But I couldn't bear to be taken out of this small beleaguered place, and if occupation lasts a long time, one international in it for the long term is more useful than one who got arrested five minutes after the soldiers arrived. I should probably decide this before the moment arrives for fight or flight. And I probably won't.

Now I'm going to undo all the good work of the herbal tea by smoking (in Arabic they say 'drinking') *shisha* with the Disaster lads amongst the broken glass of the next door Red Crescent social centre.

Fatima from Jabalia replied to me today: 'hello dear, we're fine, but the rest of the family r at [UNRWA temporary accommodation] schools and my father-in-law is at the area of the incursion and he's still alive but there is no exactly news about him. Many thanks for ur efforts to help us.'

I've texted several friends and received no replies. I remind myself of what intense strain the Jawwal phone network must currently be under.

JANUARY 12–14

Last night, Monday, at about 5am, one of our calls was to Jazeera Hotel in Al Mina (the port area) which had been shelled by Israeli ships, five minutes walk from where I live. When we first arrived it seemed there was no-one there, but eventually the medics retrieved the two caretakers from under the rubble. Fifty year old Faieq Moshtaha had shrapnel injuries but was able to walk and was put into our accompanying ambulance, 33 year old Helmi Moshtaha had shrapnel injuries and a deep head wound and was stretchered into my ambulance.

I filmed the first bit of this but then had to stop to help staunch bleeding; they might post the footage on the ISM website but it's not the best quality (my voiceover sounds like I'm stoned, but it is just lack of sleep!). Living by the sea, I know the shells are usually followed by another lot of shells five minutes later, and I was really thinking the medics were going to get hit before they got Faieq and Helmi out, but all was well. As I held a compress to Helmi's head I noticed something strange. If you have a woodburning stove, like I do, you often toast yourself mildly, and the hairs on your hand go all crisp. All of the hair on Helmi's head was like that.

Tonight, Tuesday, just before I came on shift, I caught a ride with Musa that turned unexpectedly into the pickup of the body of a resistance fighter. This was in fact the first time in all these days that I saw a fighter in my ambulance. Since it was just the two of us I helped to haul what was left of him – which didn't involve a head or the top of his torso – onto the stretcher. I was glad of the darkness that blurred the details, though it also made me very aware that our every move in this apparently empty wasteland was probably being observed. Back at the hospital I discovered that in the basement there is a man who washes and dries any of your clothes that have got blood on, within an hour.

For the medics here, it seemed this episode meant I had crossed some sort of line that brought me a little closer to their own lives. Several asked me if I had been afraid, and I gave the answer I've given you, but with the increasing feeling that not to be afraid is meaningless when it's probably down to an unawareness of what awful things *can* happen. I have started to answer apologetically, 'I'm not afraid, but I'm sure I should be.' Later on into the night, medic Aban asks me more specifically what I had felt when seeing the *shaheed* resistance guy. I think about it for a while and reply, 'I think my strongest feeling is that I am very sad that people can do this to each other. Any human to any other human, no matter what reason. And, I feel respect for the strength of someone who does this job.'

He begins to talk to me about his own feelings. He is 36, has been a medic for ten years. He has a wife and four children. He says he has never seen anything as bad as now. And he says a lot of the time he is very frightened. Sometimes so frightened, if the area is dangerous, that he almost can't bring himself to continue to drive towards the call-out location. He describes a call-out during the night that we had both been on (perhaps thinking I had observed this hesitation) saying that he first thought he couldn't do it; he had to stop, talk himself through his fear, and then continue with the collection, expecting a rocket to blow him apart at any moment. It seems that with the drone surveillance technology, they really can send rockets with your name on.

Arafa was a good friend of his, he told me, and described phoning Arafa's wife several times since his death. He tries to talk to her but she can't stop crying.

His family worry about him very much; when he visits his parents his father begs him to take a different job. But this job is important to him and he knows someone must do it. He tells me that if he came across an injured Israeli he would treat him with the same care he would anyone.

I want to hear more, but it's at this point that, in true Palestinian style, some of the others start getting distressed that there is hot food next door and I am not there eating it. It isn't good enough that I can come and have some later, or that some can be put aside for me; it doesn't matter that this is an important conversation, I am A Guest And I Must Eat Now.

Tonight, we collect two men carrying a little girl of 13 months. She is still warm, but Ishaq finds no pulse. If I understood correctly, she has had breathing difficulties since she was born, and in the rocket attack that just happened, her mother held her so tight she wasn't able to get enough air. I ask to clarify this story several times because I want to think I've misunderstood.

At one point tonight I come out of the Disaster Management room and am confronted with a family of about twelve small children, one old women, and a couple of young women, all on one sofa and all looking at me with mute appeal. The effect is so overwhelming I have to retreat back into the Disaster room again. Ambulance convoys were allowed to come up from Rafah today, and it seems this family caught a ride; whether they're here to return home or to stay with relatives because Rafah is under attack is unclear. Shortly after we load them all into an ambulance and drive them to their destination.

This appears to be a bit of town that our driver considers extremely dangerous. They have all started smiling, yet he is getting more and

more stressed, and the fact that they are all shouting directions at him
does not help. We manage to suppress all but one set of directions, and
then tip the family out at their door, trying to do it all at top speed.
Our driver screeches off, shouting in one-part jest and three-parts panic
that we are crazy to be here at all, that look! there isn't even a cat or
dog on these streets, they have too much sense, that this is all a game
to the Israelis, a computer game, that we and our ambulance are just
blips on their computer screens, that they'll destroy us just for fun.

In the light of dawn, we collect an old woman and a young man
from a shelled building down near Gaza beach; I clean the young man's
head wound. A couple of times tonight, I've looked round for a medic
and realised I'm it.

By the way – it turns out the triplets (Abdullah, Mohammad, and
little girl Samih) are about 28 days old, and have been separated from
their family ever since birth. They needed hospital care at first, but
now could go home – except their home is in Khan Younis, which is
cut off. Their poor mother is phoning every day. They are getting great
care here, but an incubator is a poor replacement for a mother's arms.

JANUARY 15

I wake into early daylight; it is Thursday morning, and the others near
me are also rousing. As I put my shoes on, my father phones, and I tell
the lads I will catch them up. I stand beside the window, overlooking
the ambulance drop-off area beside A&E. It is hard to be reassuring
when my words keep being drowned by noise. A small ginger cat skids
into the room, then climbs warily to sit at the window, peering out to
watch the street with me.

Crash! I turn around. There are flames outside the window behind
me, something has landed on the outside roof of the basement area.
'Have to go Dad, the hospital's on fire,' I say, not the best way to sign
off. I go into the hall; decide to try shouting 'Fire!' in English instead

of spending several seconds remembering the Arabic; it works just fine. I get the impression the Disaster Team boys have been on the case for some time. Several people dash in the right direction; I head for the ground floor fire hose; it won't reach, but there are buckets to be filled and I join in. Carrying a bucket to the other windows adjoining the fire, I realise it is only a few metres from the baby incubator room where the triplets are. I can stand just inside their door and watch the doctors and nurses pour pots and pans of water from the sink out the window. It seems to make little difference to the fire. White phosphorus fire does not respond to water. But we don't know that.

As I fill buckets, I gather snatches of information. More than 50 hits around us during the night, someone says. The hospital complex has been hit directly at least four times, someone else says. Tanks are round the corner. Israeli snipers are in the buildings opposite; a medic cautiously takes me to the front door and points out the window where one has been spotted, then hustles me back in, since a sniper who you can see can obviously also see you. Al Quds and the Red Crescent have received more than 150 calls for emergency help from Tel al Howa people, and cannot answer a single one.

Between buckets, several of us do decide to duck out the back of the hospital just for a few minutes, to walk a family from the building immediately behind across the few feet of dust to the shelter of Al Quds. I untie my hair; maybe it will be more obvious to watching Israelis that there is an international present. If they care at all.

It is late morning. One of the hospital staff comes in carrying pieces of a rocket that came through the wall into the pharmacy room. Others have been fighting another fire caused by a strike on the roof of the middle building, the social centre. I go via the basement and find a big hole in the lower roof, smoking rubble all over the floor which hospital workers are still trying to quench, pools of water everywhere, and an exhausted medic friend sitting on the floor, crying. It is culturally impossible for me to hug him. I sit beside him, our feet in the water.

4.4   This missile came through the hospital wall into the pharmacy of Al Quds hospital on January 15. Patients wear masks to protect them from white phosphorus.
Palestinian Red Crescent Society

Looking up through the new hole, I see the third building, the cultural centre which housed a theatre. There is nothing that can be done for it; it is burning down.

Neta from the ISM office in the West Bank gets through on the mobile. I try to pass some facts on to her; in the middle of the conversation I hear shouting from upstairs; we run. At the hospital door is Musa. He is covered in blood. 'People are running to the hospital,' he says. 'Snipers are shooting them. I carried a little girl...shot in the face...' He stands frozen, looking down at his blood-covered clothes. I realise I am still clutching the phone. The last thing I was telling Neta was that the Red Cross had instructed the Red Crescent that the Israeli army was not agreeing to rescue work of any kind so workers must not leave the hospital building.

'Neta,' I say. 'They are shooting the children. We have to go out now.' 'We'll press release,' says Neta, and I hang up. Nobody needs to think for a moment, every Red Crescent person within earshot has begun heading towards the front steps. A man is climbing them, he falls; we catch him and help him to the door. The father of the little girl. He is shot in the leg and abdomen. His wife follows, she is shouting for help – there is another daughter lost, left behind – Musa is beside me, so is Saud, we go into the street as she calls out directions after us. Twelve year old Jasmeen Batran is hiding in a house just around the corner, too terrified to move, having seen her sister and father shot. Musa puts her on his shoulders, we bring her in. Her sister has been rushed into surgery. We realise they are just the beginning of a stream of desperate people fleeing their buildings, many of which are on fire, so we return to the street, which is all the more frightening because we cannot see a soldier, we cannot see a single gun.

What do we have? Well, we have our Red Crescent vests, and watching these boys in their early twenties risking their lives, I am proud to be wearing one. After the Red Cross communication, I don't believe the army will respect the vests, but I do know that the sight of us will reassure terrorised people who are going to do this anyway. '*Fish tanziiq!*' we call to the people we are meeting, 'there is no co-ordination. We have no permission for this evacuation.' Our presence does not offer you safety.

These minutes, or hours – I cannot tell you which – are a strangely calm time. Saud pairs up with me, quietly says my name and directs me where we need to go, at first with our hands in the air but soon holding children and blankets and old people. I see men crying, children wanting to run from sheer terror and their parents gripping them tight, women clutching babies buried in blankets as if that might stop the bullets. Some wave strips of white material; makeshift white flags. We carry several people on stretchers, stopping to bandage the sniper wound of one man on the way.

At some point, Neta gets through again and says that ISM have press-released that Al Quds is being attacked and civilians are being shot and an international volunteer is present documenting. In response, many Israeli citizens are calling the army and demanding that the attacks stop. ISM have also called the Australian consulate, the consulate have called the Israeli army, and the army have said they'll stop shelling in half an hour. They don't. It will be days before they stop. But, despite expecting the crack of a bullet every moment, I witness no further sniper shooting.

We shepherd everyone to the hospital, and eventually the stream of people becomes a trickle again. Saud realises that we don't have his best friend Atif. He isn't answering his phone, and his building is closest to where the tanks are. Saud and I decide to go to get him, and after an eerie walk through emptiness, we find ourselves within a hundred yards of the tanks. A glimpse is enough; we keep moving. There is no sign of soldiers; just these solid immoveable-looking machines, lurking on the street where the children normally play. From the next building we call across, and discover several families remain in Atif's building but want to leave. First they can't find Atif, but then they do – and I swear he's slept through the whole thing, with a tank nearly under his window and deafening shelling going on. We all get back safe.

It is afternoon, and now we have about 500 frightened people in a hospital that can't feed them or give them beds or even guarantee their safety. Dr Basher is worrying this will end up like the Israeli army's siege of the Church of the Nativity in 2002 in Bethlehem, where resistance fighters and clergy and locals all ended up surrounded by the Israeli army for weeks, resorting to eating leaves. No-one kids themselves we'd be treated differently just because no fighters are taking shelter here (for obvious reasons, neither international law nor the Red Crescent allow this) – not when the snipers are shooting children. Hospital staff begin to hand out face masks, as a slightly reassuring but probably entirely ineffectual measure against breathing in white phosphorus fumes. The Red Cross is negotiating with Israel to allow an evacuation of the hospital. We are going to walk out into the street, the street where people have just been shot, and take everyone to a safe place. Well, a safer place. Well, an UNRWA school, more than a mile away.

The ground floor of the hospital is packed with people clutching blankets and children. There are not many men; it seems the Israeli army has gone into many residential buildings, rounded them up and taken them away. Red Crescent Engineer May is here with her daughter; her husband was taken. Being foreign, apparently I look like I know things. 'Do you know where my son is? My husband?' people ask me. 'My mother cannot walk. How can she come in the evacuation?' I don't know anything.

When we finally emerge cautiously onto the street, Israel has granted permission for us to use our two ambulances. That's all. A Red Cross jeep has arrived to escort us. I carry someone's bundle in one arm and hold the hand of someone's child in another. We go at the pace of the slowest, which is good because many of the smallest children prefer to stumble along clutching the skirts of their mothers; try to pick them up and they will scream – unfamiliar arms are just one more thing to fear today. The little girl I walk with tugs my arm, sobbing quietly, trying to hurry me; she doesn't know where she is going, just that she wants to be anywhere other than the street.

Explosions continue on either side. We are shocked by the thick, black cloud of smoke rising to our right. I guess it is the Islamic University; it has already been targeted several times. Siham, who I am walking with, assumes the same; I ask what she does and she answers somewhat doubtfully, looking at the cloud of smoke, that she studies journalism there. 'But maybe not anymore...' Later we find out that it is not the university burning this time, but the UNRWA depot, bombed with phosphorus. When we finally arrive at the UNRWA school, it is mostly without lighting and the black smoke still dominates the sky above. It does not feel like a place of safety. Many people make their own arrangements to go to other places, family or friends. The ones with no choice vanish into the dubious shelter of the dark, cold buildings.

I go with Atif to his friends' apartment. My phone begins to work again and I give interviews one after the other, clutching the tea Atif's friends have handed me, fearing I am making little sense. Atif tries to persuade me not to go back to hospital; but for me there is no question. Walking to Al Shifa we serendipitously find Musa driving one of the ambulances, ready to head back to Al Quds. I catch a glimpse of Ewa and Caoimhe riding with a Jabalia ambulance.

At Al Quds civilians are still sheltering; some chose not to join the walking evacuation and some have arrived since. We have about 40 patients. Explosions continue. Time shifts.

Shouting. The middle building has been bombed again and the roof is on fire. The flames are spreading swiftly. Musa grabs me and we run to the ambulance, I have no idea why. It turns out we are driving at top speed to the Civil Defence base; they have fire engines and the hospital's communications are down. Screeching to a halt outside Civil Defence, Musa has a shouted exchange out the window with the nearest people, and then we tear off again. He explains that they are saying (accurately) that without 'co-ordination' with Israel, the fire engines are likely to be bombed as they try to reach the hospital. His opinion of this is exemplified by the fact that he has just taken the ambulance out, and is now taking it back, without this same co-ordination. 'Of course Red Cross are trying to get co-ordination for the fire engines,' he says, 'but meanwhile the hospital is burning down!'

Back at Al Quds, evacuation is underway. I check for the babies; they are gone. I check each floor, loading myself up with blankets; it's cold outside. On each floor bed-ridden patients are being wheeled into lifts by calm and swiftly moving staff, most younger than me. The flames in the middle building are reaching out for our building, which holds the wards, and as I run downstairs, every landing window is manned by a Disaster Team member with a hose; I pass Saud doing his best with one and he gives me a brief smile. I hope they are at least holding the fire at bay, because it doesn't appear to be diminishing at all. I reach the basement; next door to the office of the obstetrician I was interviewing

4.5   Al Quds hospital burns as patients are evacuated into the street in their beds, January 15.

Palestinian Red Crescent Society

earlier, the roof has fallen in and the room is burning. There is no-one else here and I look round for a fire extinguisher but they are all in use elsewhere. A medic runs past; he says everyone is to get out now.

We are on the street. Again. Wearing probably useless face masks. Surrounded by explosions. Again. This time not only with elderly people and children, but people so sick the staff are carrying their beds down the front stairs. And again, everyone is thinking the next bomb will be especially for us, cowering here in the dark, with two ambulances and nowhere to go. And bits of burning debris are falling off the roof. So we start walking. At the pace of the slowest person; pushing along in hospital beds all the people we can't fit into the accompanying ambulances.

I don't know how much time has passed when the cavalry arrives; a convoy of various vehicles with wailing sirens. It seems Red Cross has obtained permission from Israel for us to be rescued. Fire trucks pass us, heading for the hospital, where they start to fight the fire. And more ambulances, which park up beside our straggling convoy and gather inside as many frightened people as they can fit. But there are a lot of us, and few of them, and those left behind as one ambulance after another leaves begin to panic, pleading with the medics for places. They are desperate to get their children off the street, out of the night, out from underneath the bombs and the gas. It seems to take forever. Finally it's only staff and volunteers left, clutching bits of computers and medical equipment, standing in the road beside the now-abandoned hospital beds. I catch a ride in the last vehicle, a van. A young nurse is sobbing and insisting we let her go back for something. One of the lads goes with her; she gathers up some files left in the middle of the road. We leave.

Some of the patients are going to Al Shifa, where there is no room for them. Some are going to the Red Cross building, I think, where there are no facilities for them. I don't know where the staff are going, I don't think they know either. At the Red Cross building, for some unknown reason, are some of my ISM colleagues. I don't really take their presence in.

I am disoriented, and disproportionately relieved when I discover five of the Al Quds volunteers are going back to the hospital. It is full of medicines and resources and machines that Gaza needs, and they, and I, don't want to leave it to the IOF. So once again, though I cannot recall how, I return to Al Quds. It occurs to me there's a chance the Israeli army will simply finish it off tonight. The volunteers wade through the water-filled corridors, collecting dry bedding. The firefighters are still fighting the fire, which they twice think they have put out, yet it keeps reviving. The Red Crescent director stands watching. It is 3am, Friday January 16. I make them all tea.

5

JANUARY 17–FEBRUARY 2, 2009

Aftermath

JANUARY 17

I found it surprisingly destabilising having to evacuate the hospital. Since the strikes began, I have spent more nights here than anywhere else, and it began to feel like coming 'home' each time I arrived, especially with the welcome I unfailingly received. There is a sense of order in a hospital, of safety and care and compassion. When a handful of us came back to mind the hospital at about 3am after evacuation, with the remains of the fire still resisting the fire-fighters, it felt very bleak. Beds were scattered in the road; inside, things were overturned and broken after the hurried leaving, the place was covered with mud. In most rooms there were waterfalls. Two out of three of our buildings were blackened and smouldering.

I wandered about in the operations room, clearing things up so it wouldn't look so sad. If I felt displaced, when I had a perfectly good flat to go to, what about all the medical folks here whose homes have been destroyed in the last weeks, for whom this was their only warm, comfortable, safe place?

But yesterday the Red Crescent met and decided they wanted to work from Al Quds again, and even better, the hospital will be open on Monday. I forgot to allow for the fact that they have no choice. Today I arrived to a completely revived atmosphere on the ground floor – lights working again, most things back in place, mud washed away, and Disaster Team boys sliding around their room on a cloth to dry their floor. I haven't been to visit the bits of the hospital that were burning two days ago. Right now I think I'll just enjoy what I see. Some of the medics are making us a potato chip dinner. The triplets are now at Nasser Children's Hospital.

Last night they bombed another UNRWA school in which homeless people had taken refuge in Beit Lahia. There are multiple wounded, including children. Two boys aged 3 and 8 are dead. John Ging of UNRWA was on the TV being coldly furious. But in the next few hours apparently a truce will begin. It is strangely quiet. Everyone desperately wants to hope it'll have some meaning.

JANUARY 18

The planes are still buzzing overhead, but there have been no explosions near me today. However this supposed ceasefire from Israeli's side since 2am does not seem to have extended to Beit Hanoun, where there was shelling this morning and F16s attacking.

This morning the Al Quds Red Crescent headed out to Zaytoun, to the area where we had a few approved evacuations and far more refused ones. Local people had already begun excavating the rubble of the Samouni house. Yesterday I helped correct the English of some of the survivor testimonies that the Red Crescent was collecting. One of the more harrowing images was a trapped and injured child describing the only food being tomatoes covered in the blood of his family, and having to sleep on their corpses amidst the rubble for three days. My nurse friend Raja at the hospital said treating one of the children that they got out in the evacuation was the first time she couldn't help but cry. He was begging her for food and water which she had to deny him until his injuries were assessed.

5.1   The dead of the Samouni family are evacuated by medics and neighbours on January 18.

Sharyn Lock

Anyway, today we arrived in the devastated Zaytoun area, where medics, friends and family began to remove the bodies of the Samounis from a hole in the roof of their flattened home. During the hour we were there, they brought up a body every ten minutes, seven in total, and I believe locals brought up at least two more after the Red Cross told us to take those we had to Al Shifa and withdraw, as a further army incursion threatened. A relative was clutching a list of 25 names of the dead.

Thank you to the brave Bristol and Brighton people for their direct action decommissioning of the EDO arms factory in Moulscome

5.2   After the house they sheltered in was attacked, Samouni family members called desperately for help for the injured, but Israel would not permit rescue.

Sharyn Lock

yesterday – it supplies parts which go into Lockheed Martin US-made F16s which are then sold to Israel. The team made a video beforehand to explain their actions: 'Israel are committing a gross crime now in Gaza. Israel have killed hundreds of children. It's absolutely disgusting that weapons made in our cities and in our country are being used to kill innocent women and children. They have been used indiscriminately. If the law and the police can't do something about it, it's time somebody else did.' Their YouTube footage shows EDO computers flying out the window – a beautiful sight. And they will all face prison.

The EDO decommissioners

On the 17th January 2009, as the bombs rained down on Gaza, six people entered the EDO factory in Brighton. They threw computers and filing cabinets out of a first floor window and took hammers to machinery used for weapons production. Their aim was to disable the war machine and to take action against those who profit from the aerial bombardment of Gaza. The arms companies who knowingly supplied the weapons to enable the invasion to happen are complicit in those crimes. (smashedo.org)

The six activists who broke into the factory were charged with conspiracy to commit criminal damage, and another three people were also charged in connection with the action, with one of the nine kept on remand from his January arrest and a predicted trial date of spring 2010. Their position was that they had lawful excuse to disarm the factory because EDO was complicit in war crimes.

In arguing this, the EDO decommissioners followed in the footsteps of the Seeds of Peace Ploughshares activists, Andrea Needham, Lotta Kronlid, Joanna Wilson and Angela Zelter, who in 1996 were cleared of causing £2million worth of damage to a British Aerospace hawk jet destined for the Indonesian airforce during the occupation of East Timor, and more recently the B52 Two, Philip Pritchard and Toby Olditch, who in March 2003 entered RAF Fairford and attempted to disarm a US B-52 bomber bound for Iraq.

References: www.smashedo.org.uk; Michael Randle, 'Direct action: A threat to democracy?' Bradford University Peace Studies Working Papers #5, 2002; www.b52two.org

JANUARY 19

We have a chance to breathe. People are out on the streets. Some shops are open. I have so much I want to write, and I'm just too tired and have no concentration. Somehow it's got to be 11pm already, so I think maybe I should go and sleep. But then there will just be more to write about tomorrow… the world just keeps turning. I want to convey some of the cautious hope I am seeing. But instead it seems like the enormity of these last days has hit me.

JANUARY 20

I woke today to the sound of shelling from Israeli ships at sea. I'm not sure they really get this ceasefire concept, though of course the bombardment is nothing like it was. In the port area on Saturday night, we had fliers dropped saying something like:

> Israel will unilaterally stop attacks at 2am Sunday Jan 18. We won't retreat from our Gaza positions, and we will respond to any Hamas attacks. Don't come near us. Don't go near Hamas positions. We don't attack civilians, only Hamas... you have to know quiet will bring quiet. You have the choice.

Uhuh.

I found a particularly farcical bunch of fliers dropped from the air into my friend's garden from about a week ago. I double checked one with head nurse Khalid. He said it was mostly about how Israel was gonna get Hamas and get them good, and it finished with:

> We will get them anywhere they are and in every way possible. For your safety, please evacuate your homes and go to the city centre.

'Where is your friend's house?' Khalid asked me.

'In the city centre,' I said. 'Just up the road from one of those city centre safe havens, an UNRWA school.'

But anyway, nothing is falling on us from the sky, currently. Today, finally, our Rafah comrades made it out and we met up to be sure we were all in one piece, which had seemed pretty unlikely for a while there. We met also with Dr Assad, Dr Haider, Dr Kamal Abu Nader, and Dr Emad Khalil Abou El Khair, who are all part of the University Teachers Association and the One Democratic State Group. They have been at the forefront of the Boycott/Divestment/Sanctions Campaign to create economic pressure on Israel to end occupation. They made a press statement about this the other day, and that night Israel hit their offices with two missiles; a third hit the neighbours. That'll teach 'em.

We went with Dr Ehad, who is Professor of Microbiology at Al Azhar University, to his family home in Jabalia. The Red Cross evacuated them during the attacks, and it's just as well. His house has more holes than a sieve. He then took us for a walk to his olive and citrus orchards, which are now bulldozed into dust. They were planted by his grandfather, who was one of the first in the area to diversify from

5.3   Jabalia girls sit on a wagonload of destroyed olive trees. Families in flattened houses gathered up the wood to keep warm.

Sharyn Lock

vegetables into citrus fruit, in 1924. Dr Ehad explains that he thinks the neighbouring fields were spared and his destroyed because, although he remains politically independent from Fatah or Hamas, he is upfront about supporting the resistance fighters. Under international law it is permitted to use force to resist an occupying army.

From his house we walked up the hill to Azbet Abd Rabbo, a short distance from Fatima's house. I have no words for what we saw. The devastation stretches as far as the eye can see; this former semi-rural community is flattened. People sit in the rubble of their homes, trying to decide how they will seek shelter from the freezing night. Many have decided the first task is to collect the splintered branches of their olive trees; perhaps they can be burnt to keep warm. Amnesty International estimates more than 3,000 houses destroyed and 20,000 damaged.[1]

JANUARY 21

Today I met with my friend Reem. She is 21 and works with MercyCorps, and we met when she came to interview me after I arrived on the initial Free Gaza trip. She was so bright and sparkly then, and I know that is still in her somewhere, but right now she is very fragile. She didn't realise I was back in the country until last Thursday, when her family was one of the many fleeing to Al Quds hospital, and we collided amidst the chaos. Today she told me about what happened to them:

Tuesday night, we had stayed with my uncle elsewhere, because the attacks were so bad. But Wednesday we went home, because it was home. Also we heard that the bombs Israel was using set things on fire, and we thought if we were in our home we could put out small fires before they burnt everything. We just didn't realise how bad it was going to get.

Wednesday night was terrifying. The bombing, the shelling – my mother was shaking and reading prayers. We realised how dangerous it was there on the 5th floor, but we were too scared to go downstairs because there were windows all the way and we were afraid the Israeli soldiers would see us and shoot. My uncle lives on the ground floor, he has two daughters of 6 and 1½, my grandmother lives with him also. He called us and said, come downstairs, but we said we just can't. Next thing we knew, he'd come upstairs to get us. He actually went all the way up to the 7th floor by accident, and had to come back down to bang on our door. So we took blankets and went downstairs with him. We kept thinking – at 4am it will stop. Maybe at 6am it will stop. Because usually the army withdrew by then. We didn't realise they were just continuing to move towards us this time.

Some hours later, my aunt looked out the window and saw a tank; it was pointing directly at our windows. That's it, in a moment the shells will hit us directly, we're dead, we thought. But something happened and it turned away from us. I called MercyCorps, where I go to youth group, and asked them to call the Red Cross and ask for help. But we realised we had to escape immediately. We couldn't go back to the 5th floor for our day clothes or our passports or IDs. My brother was so worried because if the soldiers got him with no ID, they would shoot him. But everyone in our building said, we have to go NOW. But we knew the snipers had just shot a man and his daughter (Haneen Al Batran and her father).

We went outside, we had small children with us – some of the little ones could barely walk but they had to if there wasn't anyone to carry them. Then I saw you and the other Red Crescent people; my brother was helping my grandmother but she fell, and he stopped with her though he was sure he would be shot. Then you went to help them, so me and the rest of the family went on into the hospital. We waited for 10 minutes and my uncle and brother and grandmother didn't arrive, and we were sure they were dead. We checked the basement but we didn't know it had two sides. I started to cry. Mum was shouting at everyone – did you see them, did you see them?

Then I saw my brother and I shouted 'where the hell have you been!'

After some hours they said everyone would evacuate from the hospital and go to the UNRWA school, but we had to walk. It's a long way and my grandmother can't walk. But then we got a wheelchair so we could push her. I was carrying someone else's child because her parents had their other children, she was afraid not to be with them so she cried all the way; she could see how scared we all were. I realised how empty this area of the city was, everything was burning, it was a city of ghosts. I believed they would drop a bomb on us as we walked. But we arrived to the school.

From the UNRWA school, we went to my uncle's wife's relatives. We had nowhere else to go; we stayed three days. We wanted to go home, but we expected the army would shell the whole of Tel al Howa. After the army withdrew, my father and brother went to check our home and bring our passports and ID. After the ceasefire we went home. But we can still hear shelling from the sea. We think it's not really a truce, it's more just a break.

I lost my friend from the WhyNot project – Christine al-Turki. She was really dear to me, she was one of the sweetest girls, kind of smooth and soft. Her parents only had her and her brother, so they took such care of her, and gave her so many opportunities, she took lots of classes and things... she was literally scared to death. She got asthma and then a heart attack, from fear. It was Friday, the day she died. I began to think it would happen to me too, because I was scared to death too. I was so affected by that, my family tried to be very close to me to help me. I looked on Facebook, her friends made an online group for her, and the photos of her after she died affected me so much; one of her father kissing her goodbye for the last time. I couldn't believe she would never be back.

Then I heard my friend from college, Bissam – her name means 'spring' – was dead. This shock was even worse. I couldn't eat or talk. My uncle wanted to wake me out of my shock. He shouted at me – it's not the time for this – any of us might die at any moment, but we have to try to survive – show some care for yourself, for your family, wake up! I realised I had to find some strength, so I started to eat.

Some of my relatives live in Tuam. Their building was destroyed; six families lived there. My friend's home was destroyed by shells. Some other relatives had their home burnt. Then yesterday I went to MercyCorps, and I found out my friend Jihan, who worked at Sharek Youth Project, is dead. I was listening to everyone's stories and I wanted to escape from reality but it was chasing me. During the attacks, I was calling all my friends every night to say goodbye, I was saying to all of them, please forgive me for any bad things I did. And they would say, Reem, please shut up!

My friends always used to say I was like a character out of a fairy tale, like Snow White or someone, not really living in the real world. After these days, I guess I am in the real world. I can't watch the news, because the news was us, my life, my friends. All me and my family are thinking about now is leaving Gaza.

In these last days, whenever Red Crescent folks from other places turned up on ambulance runs, the greetings were much closer to reunions. Big hugs and five or six smacking kisses on each cheek. The subtext: 'you're still alive. It's a miracle, you're still alive.' Eva heard today of a third friend who is dead. She has had a hard time. I have lost no-one personal to me.

I have three hangovers that I'm aware of from these days. One, I hate to sleep alone at my flat; the two nights I did during the attacks, it felt too far from the hospital where my work and my friends were and I was worried I would be cut off from them. It still somehow feels like being in the wrong place. Two, I feel happiest when my three best Red Crescent friends are all present and within my sight. Three, in the dark, when I see bags of rubbish on the street, I think they are bodies. This is because when we went to pick up bodies lying in the dark, they really did look more like crumpled bags of rubbish than the people they had been.

On January 15, pausing at the Red Cross after hospital evacuations, I was only vaguely aware of the appearance of some of my ISM colleagues; Vik told me much later that, having spent most of the preceding 24 hours expecting me to be blown up, he asked me how I was and I completely ignored him. This led to weeks of accidental acrimony which we each thought the other started. Somehow we internationals assumed our friendships would be unaffected by the strain of these crazy days, and he and I were not the only ones to make personal what is in fact obviously environmental.

Some time after the ceasefire, we had progressed to leaving tunnel-smuggled chocolate bars for each other, since any non-chocolate-related form of communication still went wrong. One effort on his part made me smile despite its failure. 'Muskeli! Bought you very big chocolate cake. Now forgot it in taxi.'

The Arabic word for 'problem' is *muskela*, but Vik had italianised it years ago on his first West Bank trip. Delightedly, his Palestinian friends followed suit, in their best Italian accents. Even Fida started texting 'Moooskeli!' The traditional story as to why Fida's and many other Palestinian families have whole crops of children with red hair is that one hundred years ago, an Irish woman came to Gaza, and they are all her descendants. We speculated that in one hundred years' time, an Italian man will be blamed for the altered pronunciation of Arabic.

The strength of Gazan people astounds me. Everyone was out today fixing things. Re-laying water pipes, clearing rubble. Putting aside the thoughts of the children who are dead, to smile for the children who are still alive. How is it done? Where do they find the courage? And what will be their reward for getting up and going on, one more time?

Today, again, I woke to the sound of shelling from Israeli ships in the Gaza sea.

Later...

I received this email on January 18. It had been sent the day before.

Subject: Help Request Through ISM Website

I am writing to make a request for a good friend from Gaza that I have known for 5 years now, Amer Shurrab... He just found out his father and two brothers were attacked while returning home from their farm during the 3-hr ceasefire. One brother (Kassab Shurrab) died, but the father (Mohammed Shurrab, age 64) and the remaining brother (Ibrahim, age 17) are now wounded and stranded in an Israeli Defense Force controlled area. It's been 16 hours now and emergency services are unable to reach them.

The ambulances cannot travel there without permission from the IDF, and local aid groups claim that soldiers are blocking their access. We have spoken with the local Red Cross in Khan Younis and they have been trying to get the IDF's permission to get to the family, but have not been allowed. What we are asking, is if you could help by using any of your contacts to bring attention and pressure in order to get permission for the ambulances to save two lives. We are very desperate and trying as many avenues as possible to help aid reach them. If you know even an Israeli foot soldier who might be able to push the ball by calling a local commander we would really appreciate any help. His father and brother are located at: In front of Supermarket Abu Zidan El-Najar, El Fukhari (neighbourhood) Khan Younis (town) Gaza. We truly appreciate any help at this time.

I replied as follows:

Dear friends,

This is a terrible situation and there are so many similar ones from what I have heard in the last days. I am so very sorry about Kassab. I have been volunteering with the Red Crescent and infuriatingly we cannot move without Red Cross co-ordination, which Israel rarely agrees to (already more than 11 medics have been killed when they tried to rescue the wounded.) The day before yesterday we tried to get permission from Israel to collect wounded from Khan Younis and they refused.

Now I am hoping greatly that today after the ceasefire your relatives have been collected by ambulances, because in our area (Zaytoun) we were able to go into areas that before we were not allowed.

If that is not the case, please phone me, I have no idea what I can do but I will try at least to find out information if you cannot. You must be terribly worried and I am so sorry.

I am CCing Angela from Israeli Campaign against Housing Demolition who knows how to contact Israeli forces. But I am still hoping that today your relatives were collected safely.

The answer came back today.

Thank you for ur email and all your help. Help reached them during the ceasefire on Saturday, 24 hrs later. Ibrahim, 18 yrs, has passed away during that time, the father is at the European hospital now in Khan Younis. Again, we thank you, and we are very sorry for the losses all aid groups endured. Plz let me know if u need more information. We are thankful for everything.

JANUARY 22

Today we visited Al Shifa to document some of the people injured since the 'ceasefire'. Little Ahmad Hassaneen, 7, from Shuja'iyya in East Gaza, near to the border, is in a coma. He was shot in the head about 9.45am today while playing with other children. Dr Fawzi Nabusi showed us the X-ray of the bullet in his brain.

Yasser Abd, age 15, was shot in Beach camp at around 7am. He'd heard shelling from the sea, went outside to see what was happening, and was shot in the head. Two girls of 4 and 5 and a man, all from Beach camp, were hit as well.

Dr Hassan Khalif, Director of Al Shifa hospital, tells us that since the 'ceasefire', three people have been killed, and 15 injured. Ten of these were injured today on the 22nd and five of them were fishermen.

I was visiting the Kabariti family this morning during the shelling. Together we watched the gunboat from their front window, listening to the repetitive 'boom, boom, boom... thud, thud, thud'.

Later...

Ramattan TV, nine floors up and open 24 hours, was the last bastion of internet during the strikes. We knew the place because we got asked in for interviews, and then called press conferences there, for example announcing that internationals would be riding with ambulances. We began to hang around in the corners at other times, hoping no-one would mind us hitching a ride on the wi-fi.

Instead of complaining about random internationals cluttering up the place, Ramattan journalists wholeheartedly adopted us, brought us tea, gave us blankets if we needed to stay the night. Now most nights at about 9pm, you'll find some of us being fed a small feast in the kitchen.

I forgot that I didn't like journalists much, because these guys are firstly Palestinian, and their reporting is compassionate.

Yousef Al Helou has the end office in Ramattan, but actually works for Press TV. His TV speaks English sometimes, and he's always willing to pool information and help us figure out what is going on. Today he took Eva and me to Zaytoun to hear the story of his cousin's family.

When we arrived, I realised we were only two houses from the first house we'd evacuated people from on the Red Cross evacuation on January 8. I would have walked past Amer and Shireen Al Helou's house that day. But by then it was empty and broken, because the day Amer told us about was January 4.

Amer is 29. Fourteen people from his family were in the house that night, and they were all trying to sleep under their stairs as some sort of shelter. Even though the stairs were partly open to the back yard, the

5.4 The Al Helou family's house was occupied on January 4. Baby and grandfather were killed as the family fled, while daughter and uncle survived bullet wounds. The destroyed vehicle is the bread delivery van young father Amer had used to support them.

Sharyn Lock

F16 attacks on the house made downstairs seem the safest place. The house now has holes from shell blasts and thousands of pock-marks from the three-inch nails the shells were filled with.

'We hadn't known how bad it would get,' Amer told us. 'Or we would have left our house and gone somewhere else. But we thought our area was a quiet area. And then that night we thought they would go past us at the front. But they came from the back.' Amer didn't know it yet, but his brother, resistance fighter Mohammed, had already been killed elsewhere that day, struck by drone rockets.

The Israeli soldiers came at about 5.30am, after the house had been shelled for 15 hours, and immediately opened fire on the family, killing Amer's father with three shots. Then they told the family to leave. Amer had called an ambulance (which had to turn back after being shot at) and was refusing to leave his father's body but the soldiers said they would shoot him if he stayed, so the family fled 300 yards up the dirt track behind their house, at which point they were shot at again by another group of soldiers. This time Amer's brother Abdullah was shot, Amer and Shireen's 6 year old daughter Saja was shot in the arm, and their 1 year old daughter Farah was shot in the stomach. They spent the next 14 hours sheltering behind a small hill of dirt, while the wounded bled, and were not allowed to access help though the soldiers were aware of the injuries. Having no other way to comfort her small daughter, whose intestines were falling out, Shireen breastfed Farah as the little girl slowly bled to death.

After 14 hours, at about 8 in the evening, the soldiers sent dogs to chase them out of their shelter and dropped phosphorus bombs near them, but due to the wounded family members and having bare feet in an area of broken glass and rubble, escape was difficult. The army took the three wounded and put them behind the tanks, and captured Amer, but the rest of the family managed to get away and call the Red Crescent. The ambulance that eventually reached the injured people seven hours later (driven by my medic friend Musa) took an hour to find them, and by this time Farah was dead. (When I heard Amer's story I realised Musa had already told me about collecting 'a small *shaheed*' from this area.)

Amer was held for five days in army custody (the first three without access to food, water or a bathroom), beaten and tortured, and questioned about resistance activity, about which he knew nothing. When he was finally released on the border, the army sent two known collaborators to escort him, so it would look to the resistance fighters like he himself was a collaborator. But the fighters knew who he was and that he was not a collaborator. He tells us:

I had my four children young, and they gave me the most happiness in my life. I took such good care of them. I didn't let them just play on the street, we had a big living room in our house with toys for them, we would invite all the neighbours' children to come play there with ours, so that we could be sure they were all safe. I always drove them to and from school, I didn't even let them walk. Whenever I was depressed, I would gather all my kids, pile them in the car, take them somewhere nice like the park or the beach, and then to see them happy and having fun would make me happy again.

Now my remaining children will not go to sleep without their shoes on, because they think we will have to run for our lives again.

We love life as the Israelis do. Are they the only people allowed life? They killed me three times that day, first when they killed my brother, then when they killed my father, then when they killed my daughter. We looked for my father's body later; they had buried him under rubble, eventually we found his foot sticking out. Sometimes now I think we have to leave Gaza, to join my brother in South Africa. Sometimes I think, no – Gaza is worth fighting for, this is our home.

Amongst their crumpled belongings, next to the spot Amer's father died, the family gives us coffee. Shireen solicitously dusts the sand off my back. We ask them how it is they have not gone crazy from the pain of these events. 'It's not us, it's God who gives us peace and strength. Without this I would be dead too. What happened to my family was like a horror film,' says Amer. He shows us photos of Farah (whose name means 'joy') and Saja on his phone. 'I don't think I can have any more children. I am too broken inside.'

The family is not living in the house right now, they are split between different homes, and Abdullah is in hospital in Egypt. Amer is wearing Abdullah's jacket, complete with bullet holes. 'It is hard to be here again in this house after what happened. But your presence has lifted my spirits,' he tells us.

5.5   Amer and Shireen, the young couple on the right, are supported by neighbours as they clean up their bombed, occupied house. Inevitably, someone still manages to offer us coffee.

Eva Bartlett

   Back at Ramattan, I hear one of the journalists talking. 'I couldn't protect my children – this is my responsibility, and I couldn't,' he says. 'My daughter asked, what is it like to die? I told her, it's just like closing your eyes.'

JANUARY 23

Sometimes I come across quotes that go some way to explaining what was going on in the minds of the soldiers who perpetuated some of these horrors.

I believe that it should have been even stronger! Dresden! Dresden! The extermination of a city! After all, we're told that the face of war has changed. No longer is it the advancing of tanks or an organized military. [...] It is a whole nation, from the old lady to the child, this is the military. It is a nation fighting a war. I am calling them a nation, even though I don't see them as one. It is a nation fighting a nation. Civilians fighting civilians. I'm telling you that we [...] must know [...] that stones will not be thrown at us! I am not talking about rockets – not even a stone will be thrown at us. Because we're Jews. [...] I want the Arabs of Gaza to flee to Egypt. This is what I want. I want to destroy the city, not necessarily the people living within it.

Reserve Colonel Yoav Gal, an Israeli Air Force pilot, on army radio during Operation Cast Lead (January 11, 2009)

JANUARY 25

This morning is the second that I woke to quietness; no shelling from the sea. Eva and I went to see our Jabalia friends, Fatima's family. They are back in their house, one of the few standing in Azbet Abd Rabbo. This is only the case because it was again occupied by the army during the land incursion. Israeli soldiers don't clean up after themselves so the family has been cleaning for a week solid – without running water.

It was so good to be able to sit in the sun with them and drink tea and watch the children playing in the garden. I'd not seen the children in a state other than fear, nor in a location other than the basement. Abu Nasser (the husband of Sara who was killed in the first attack as she was out looking for bread) came through the whole thing ok despite refusing to leave the neighbourhood when the rest of the family did. He has been ill, not surprisingly, and was feeling chilly despite the sun. He described coming back to the house as soon as he thought it was possible, and watching the Israeli soldiers dancing as they left. He always reminds me of a wiry old fisherman, with a white beard, bright

5.6   A whole landscape of Jabalia family houses were bombed, then mined.
Sharyn Lock

eyes, and a woolly hat on. He says, and apparently other Palestinians in their eighties agree, that these attacks have been worse than anything they ever saw before. This is the fourth attack on the Jabalia area in three years.

On the way we dropped into the Jabalia Red Crescent centre that we had to evacuate on the first night of the ground incursion; one room is burnt out, it has a lot of holes in, and the windows are all broken, but it could be worse. All the guys were there working hard to clear up. Even Hassan was there, limping and still sounding a bit shell-shocked.

Our friend Abu Hozeifa took us around a part of Azbet I didn't see the other day, and we recorded some more stories. We begin with Ayman Torban's house, where he and his brother's family lived, a total of 17 people. I was immediately intrigued because under the rubble was a paper on midwifery in Palestine and I spotted more crumpled midwifery books. It turned out this was an extensive medical and science library put together by his sister Amal (her name means 'hope') who did her midwifery masters in London, and taught here in Gaza, but now lives in Dubai.

We sat in the flimsy shelter Ayman has constructed and heard what happened. He told us this house was first shelled on January 4, when only the women and children were there – in many cases the men feel their families are safer without them because of the Israeli army's tendency to regard all men as militants. He said their home was attacked with two Apache rockets and five tank shells.

Two days later the relatives realised everyone in the basement was still alive, and one of the women went to tell them it might be ok to come out. First she brought out the children, and three tanks came to confront them. But she went back, waited with the women inside for two hours, and then they all came out and reached safety.

Two days later the army went into the house and laid mines, which collapsed it completely. This was the pattern for most Jabalia houses, which appears to be why the devastation is so complete. A young man

5.7   Homeless Jabalia families create temporary shelters out of the fragments of their houses.

Sharyn Lock

sitting with us said, 'Before these attacks I wanted to travel. But now I want to stay in our land. Who will protect it if we all leave?'

Next to the Torban house are the Badwan and Ayoub houses. Maher Badwan (who had taken most of the family to his cousin's house), told us that Mousa Ayoub fled his own home and went to the Badwan house, where he hid with Maher's mother in the kitchen while the building was hit with tank shells and phosphorus. Both died; Maher's mother survived a short time but no ambulance was able to reach her. The army then planted mines in the house (black crosses on the pillars to mark the best place for them are still visible) and collapsed it with the bodies still inside.

Mahoud Abed Rabbu lived in a three floor, six apartment building. On January 6 it came under shell attack from 10.30am. At 2pm during the 1–4pm 'ceasefire', the army dynamited a wall open and told Mahoud and his family: 'Leave here, go into the town, we'll kill you if you return.' Everybody walked towards Jabalia centre, until they reached a mosque, when other soldiers took all the men – about 60 of them – and put them in an animal shelter. Women and children were allowed to leave.

They took the IDs of the men, made them strip, and then used them as human shields as they continued to dynamite houses open and enter them. Finally the army released the men at about 10pm (again warning them not to return or the army would kill them) except for ten who they arrested and who are believed to still be in the Israeli Naqab (Negev) prison.

Mousa Ayoub's neighbour Khalid Abed Rabbu told us that on the same day, three tanks surrounded his house and the soldiers shouted at him to get out. He went outside with his wife, children, and mother, carrying a white flag. He remembers noticing that two of the soldiers in the tanks were eating chocolate. A third soldier got out of the tank, and opened fire on the family with an M16. Khalid tried to take his family back into the house, but his daughters, Soad, aged 7 and Amal, aged 2, were killed. His mother received bullets in her arm and stomach. His 4 year old daughter Samar was hit with three bullets and was evacuated for intensive care in Belgium; if she survives she will be paralysed.

A few minutes away, his ambulance driver neighbour Samir Hassheikh heard Khalid's call for help and tried to bring the ambulance to them, but tanks stopped him. The army later destroyed the ambulance along with Samir's house. After two hours Khalid managed to bring his injured mother and daughter to a point another ambulance could reach. Eva remembers bringing in Khalid's mother while she was on duty with the Jabalia Red Crescent. The sadness on Khalid's face as he told us his story, sitting beside the rubble of his home, has stayed with me. I couldn't bring myself to ask to take his photo.

5.8   Reemas, Hozeifa and Abdullah, whom I first met in hiding in their Jabalia family basement.

Sharyn Lock

As we were walking the Azbet neighbourhood, I got a text from Vik: 'Israel radio says right now that they are ready to attack again today. Take care.' Wordlessly, I showed it to Eva. It took a while before we could face asking Abu Hozeifa if he knew anything. He said there had been something on the radio but everyone hoped it was just a rumour.

The children whose family we visited today spent the whole visit playing with a wheelchair, which belongs not to any of the kids, thank goodness, but to the father of the oldest boy, Abu Abdullah, who lacks both legs, yet continues to tackle life with humour and enthusiasm. It made me smile to watch them use the chair for their games. But it reminded me of something I saw before the attacks: two young friends, boys of about 12, riding down the street side by side. One was on his bike, the other in a motorised wheelchair. This is Gaza.

JANUARY 26

Back in Gaza City late last night, we met by the sea to welcome Andrew, who returned through the Rafah border the day before, after his kidnap off a Gaza fishing boat by Israel late last year. It was hard to give him much of a festive welcome with the grim stories we had to tell.

Moh spoke of the Al Fukhari area, near his home, where due to lack of electricity for radios or phones, no-one had heard a thing about the danger of the phosphorus bombs, and thought they were just fireworks. Many people went out to see what they were, and received serious burns.

And so many more stories, even just one or two steps from me.

Jilal, from Jabalia Red Crescent, who – like so many, many men – worked for ten years to afford his house, now destroyed.

Majed, my nurse friend from Al Awda hospital, whose aunt is in hospital with a fractured leg; her house fell on her.

Nurse Khalid's wife and two little daughters, alone in their small tin-roofed house in Magazi refugee camp, while he was cut off from them in Gaza City. They sheltered in the room they thought safest, but it was struck by a rocket. They moved to another room, it was struck by a second rocket. A final rocket struck the third room they tried. Now the family is living with Khalid's father.

Basma from the UHWC, who tells me about the family that called her, crying, to say they had no home and no possessions and were going to have to sleep on the street that night.

Hamse, our 21 year old security guard with whom all the other internationals (who are not so stroppy about police guards as I am) made friends. He survived the first day attacks that killed so many police, but was killed later. He leaves a 5 month old daughter.

Dr Waleed, Medical Director of Al Quds hospital; his friend now has a leg amputation with continuing complications. She had woken in the night with the feeling she should move her family out of the room they were in. But after shifting them, she went back and the room was hit.

Vik interviewed Dalal, the 12 year old whose entire family died while she was with her grandma. Her house is destroyed, all that is left her is her cat.

And Amira, who crawled, injured, to the house of my friend Haider Eid's cousin. Haider wrote about her on Electronic Intifada:

14-year old Amira Qirm, whose house in Gaza City was shelled with artillery and phosphorus bombs – bombs which burnt to death 3 members of her immediate family: her father, her 12-year-old brother, Ala'a, and her 11-year old sister, Ismat. Alone, injured and terrified, Amira crawled 500m on her knees to a house close by – it was empty because the family had fled when the Israeli attack began. She stayed there for 4 days, surviving only on water, and listening to the sounds of the Israeli killing machine all around her, too afraid to cry out in pain in case the soldiers heard her. When the owner of the house returned to get clothes for his family, he found Amira, weak and close to death.

When I saw Khalid the other day, on the request of a journalist, I asked him about evidence of the weapon called 'dime' bombs. He said the ICU doctors were seeing something new to them: what appeared to be mild external shrapnel injuries coupled with disproportionate massive internal damage. 'There will be small chest wounds, but then the lungs will be destroyed. Or minor abdominal entry wounds but then kidneys and liver destroyed.'

I didn't manage to finish writing this last night, and a quiet night made me hopeful. But just now, 11.45am, we heard an explosion some distance from where I am sitting in the Red Crescent office. Eva, who had earlier reported the return of planes over the city, called to say it had rocked her building. I have on my lap the small son of one of the medics, a quiet child of a little over a year, who is wearing a thoughtful expression. What will happen to us all if this begins again?

One of the incredibly frustrating things about the last weeks was Israel deliberately attacking ambulances and killing medical workers who went to collect the wounded, resulting in the Red Cross instructing the Red Crescent not to move unless permission from Israel was in place. In the final days of attacks, Caoimhe and Ewa decided several times to move without permission (or 'co-ordination' as the Red Cross calls it) along with a couple of intrepid medics. So around the same time as my hospital was on fire, they were going to some houses where five men had tried to go outside to get bread for their children. The men's bodies were now in pieces on their doorsteps, within view of hysterical wives and children. Ewa and Caoimhe went in with stretchers, collected the body pieces, and evacuated the families.

JANUARY 27

Yesterday Eva and I went back to see Amer at his Zaytoun house. He told us his brother Abdullah is back home from the Egyptian hospital, and showed us his hospital records; his wounds (two shots to abdomen,

DIME munitions

Rumours of brutal new weaponry spread like wildfire in war zones. Amongst the suspicions that emerged from Gaza during Operation Cast Lead were the use of depleted uranium (DU) weapons and Dense Inert Metal Explosives (DIME) munitions.

However, according to investigations and tests carried out by Human Rights Watch (HRW) and information from NGOs accumulated by the International Coalition to Ban Uranium Weapons (ICBUW), it seems unlikely that either of these munitions were used in Gaza, although other modified weaponry probably was.

A statement released by ICBUW in July 2009, reads:

> To date, we believe that there is still no compelling evidence to support the claim that Israel used uranium weapons in the attack. This is likely to remain the case until independent sampling is undertaken and the results published.

ICBUW concluded that rumours of DU use resulted from suspicions that Boeing's GBU-39 Small Diameter Bombs had been used to collapse tunnels on the border between Gaza and Egypt. However, HRW investigations suggested it was unlikely that GBU-39s had been used, as the sandy soil and un-reinforced structures of the tunnels made specialist munitions unnecessary. Boeing also stated that although it had received an Israeli order for GBU-39 bombs, it had yet to deliver them, and although DU was included on the patent list of possible materials for use in GBU-39s, its manufacturing plant did not have a licence to use it.

After liaising with HRW and specialists from the Mines Advisory Group, ICBUW also determined that allegations that Israeli tanks fired DU rounds probably referred to High Explosive Anti-Tank (HEAT) rounds.

Rumours that Israeli forces had been using DIME munitions initially seemed more convincing. These are missiles with warheads packed with high explosives and powdered tungsten, designed to produce a very intense but localised blast.

▶

According to ICBUW:

The first reliable reports that something was amiss came from doctors working for the Norwegian humanitarian NGO NORWAC. They were observing unusual injuries in the survivors of attacks by drones. The injuries were massive and unlike any they had come across in their years of experience working in combat zones... Subsequent testing of fragments by Human Rights Watch and NORWAC, analysis of blast patterns and eyewitness reports led them to conclude that what they were seeing was the use of fragmentation sleeves on drone-launched missiles.

Rather than DIME weapons, therefore, HRW considered that the Israeli military was adding a sleeve made from tiny tungsten cubes onto Spike missiles, turning them 'into an effective anti-personnel weapon. The cubes spread outward from the blast site and act as micro-shrapnel.'
ICBUW ended its July statement by calling for 'the long-term monitoring of civilians with embedded tungsten micro-shrapnel from Israeli missiles due to concerns over the carcinogenicity of tungsten'.

References: ICBUW, 'July statement on the alleged use of uranium weapons in Gaza in January 2009'; HRW, 'Precisely wrong: Gaza civilians killed by Israeli drone-launched missiles, June 2009.

one to arm) are healing ok. He was worried about Saja, his 6 year old, though, as he thought the gunshot wound to her arm wasn't healing properly, and he wasn't sure if he could get an overworked doctor's attention under current circumstances. Eva had links with doctors at Al Wafa hospital in Shuja'iyya, where the Helou family are staying with Shireen's sister's family, so she called Dr Tariq and asked if he would see Saja the next day.

Amer has a lot of friends dropping by when he is at his Zaytoun house; they don't want him to be alone. One of the young men here lost his brother, as Amer lost Mohammed. Amer told us Mohammed's wife is four months pregnant.

One of the friends made us a wonderful *makluba* dish for lunch, with virtually no facilities. Eva told us how she thought this was solely the name of this chicken and rice dish, and couldn't understand what it meant when someone said his room was all *makluba*. It just means 'upside down'. Luckily while we ate, the wind was blowing the right way. When it's blowing the wrong way, everyone still trying to live in a semi-rural area like this has to deal with the aroma of rotting chickens, cows, and sheep, killed or starved during the attacks.

Today Eva and I met Amer and Saja in the Shuja'iyya market to go to Al Wafa rehabilitation hospital. Saja is a finely boned child with a solemn face, who kept close to her dad, sitting as far forward on the taxi's back seat as she could in order to be near him in the front seat. When you remember that she saw her grandad and baby sister killed, it's not surprising. She was sucking a lollipop and wasn't willing to open her mouth to say a word for some time. When we got back to her home later and she was with her relatives and her little brother Mohammed (her other brother Foad was at kindergarten) she relaxed and drew some pictures for us.

Dr Tariq is a kind man, but Saja was suspicious, and she had reason, as the examination of her arm unavoidably had her crying with pain. The wound has healed on the outside, but there may be some internal problems, and a further operation might be required.

I learnt in my early visits to Palestine not to show admiration for anything that Palestinians have that they could physically give to you, because they will. I try to limit my compliments to things that are bolted down, and children. But I slipped up today... when Shireen arrived, Eva and I both commented on how much we like her clothes, and that we'd like her to show us where she finds them. She immediately went into the back of the house and came back with two of her shirts, one each, for which she would accept no refusal.

By the end of the visit, we'd also collected a commemorative Palestine sash from one of her friendly family members, and some high energy biscuits from the World Food Programme, which were apparently a

'Gift of Norway' before they were a gift of Shireen. I felt that I wasn't really keeping up my end of things with the *halva* I'd brought, but it made Shireen smile, because Amer had yesterday joked that my bag had a supermarket in it, after I'd pulled out cashew nuts followed by *maramiya* (sage) for the tea.

We asked Amer about work. He said that before the attacks he delivered bread in his own delivery van, but he couldn't do this job anymore. We understood; we had seen the remnants of the van outside the Zaytoun house.

Eva and I said that we would let folks who read our blogs know they can make donations to go towards medical treatment Saja might need, if they would like. She'll be assessed on Thursday. I *think* we can convince Amer and Shireen to accept this; after several battles over several days I managed to pay for our taxi today by saying 'It's not my money, but donations from people outside that I'm paying with.' (It's actually a bit of both. I hope Amer doesn't read this. He has a sneaky way of shaking hands with the driver and simultaneously passing shekels over when we're not looking.)

While we were at Al Wafa, there was gunfire about every five minutes. Apparently the army constantly firing over the border is normal there. This is another hospital that was attacked. We examined a ward room with a huge shell hole in it. There were normally three patients in this room, but luckily this side of the building had been evacuated when the rocket went in one wall, through the room, and out the other.

While we were there, Eva took me to meet Abd, whose case she took up when she was in Egypt. He's 18 now, and he was shot by a sniper in the March 2008 invasion. He had gone up on the house roof to find out why there was no water from their tank (that was also because of sniper shot, it turned out). He was shot in the spine, and it was a little while before his family realised he was missing. He was sent to Egypt for treatment, and was in a pretty bad way when Eva met him, emaciated, with bed sores, cut off from his family, and having been shifted round five Egyptian hospitals.

The advice Eva was given was to try to arrange his removal back to Gaza, which surprised her because of the siege conditions, but then she learnt about the good quality long-term care for rehabilitation patients that is available at Al Wafa. She played a key part in getting Abd home, and he is now greatly improved physically and has had some visits home. However, the three solicitous doctors clustered round his bed were telling us that he is very dispirited.

It seems to have hit him that he will never walk, and he is grieving for the life he won't have. Al Wafa staff are doing their best to show him the life he *can* have. How many more young people must there be like him after these last weeks, with so much lost. We wondered if we could ask Eva's friend Abu Abdullah to visit Abd. Abu Abdullah lost both his legs, but he is a very strong, positive, and witty man.

JANUARY 29

On Saturday January 17, with rumours of an imminent ceasefire reaching the rural Beit Hanoun borderland, Manwar and her 22 year old daughter Sharifa dared to believe their house had miraculously survived the war. There were dead, injured, and homeless among their neighbours; everyone's cropland was pitted with F16 bomb craters and covered with poisonous phosphorus; wells were smashed. Sheep and goats were rotting under houses deliberately destroyed with the animals still inside. But Manwar and Sharifa's house still stood, amongst tall palms, within sight of Israel, and despite their fear and isolation they'd determinedly not left it.

And then, at 2.30pm, the inevitable happened. Four Israeli tanks and one enormous military bulldozer came for the few houses still standing; squeezing in the final demolishing before the ceasefire came into effect. 'I was so scared when I saw the tanks. My heart dropped to my feet,' says Manwar. The soldier with the megaphone shouted for anyone inside the house to get out of what they announced was now

– illegally – a closed military zone. As Sharifa left she told them there were no men inside; the soldiers refused to believe two women alone could have stayed through three weeks of attacks. 'Walk towards Gaza,' they were told, refusing Manwar's request for time to gather a few possessions. From a distance, Manwar watched her house bulldozed; she and Sharifa joining the approximately 400 people in Beit Hanoun who've lost their houses and livelihoods to this new 'buffer zone'.

5.9   ISM group meets Manwar to accompany her to rescue belongings from the rubble of her house, Beit Hanoun.

Sharyn Lock

Today we and local Palestinian activists join the family to walk back to the mangled house on the little hilltop, in the danger zone. Manwar hopes to retrieve some documents, photos, anything really. As we walk through this green valley, we imagine the orange and lemon orchards that once meant there were loads of jobs here; Israel destroyed these long ago.

Sifting through rubble is as dispiriting as I imagined. We carefully retrieve what fragments we can of the family's life, knowing each dust-covered item of clothing, unbroken bowl, or piece of paper may have a value heightened by the impossibility of reaching the rest, buried under concrete slabs we can't move. We split up to assist the neighbours in the same way. Their home was even simpler, almost Bedouin style. These families lived at subsistence level. It is not long before 'warning bullets' begin to whizz past our ears in both locations, from the Israeli base across the fence.

Well, there's not much more that can be retrieved without unavailable heavy machinery, so we begin the walk back, passing many other 'pancaked' houses. Sharifa has brought the horse and cart to meet us, and Manwar climbs aboard, carefully loading the tattered plastic bags of what we were able to rescue of her life. She is beaming.

JANUARY 31

Wednesday/Thursday, January 14/15, was the worst night for the people in Tel al Howa. I've already told Reem's story. It was also the night they began to drop rockets on Al Quds hospital, with our worst rocket fire occurring Thursday night.

Today I met Majda Nadeem and her children. They live on the third floor of a building beside the crossroads of the main road that leads from Al Quds hospital. I was led to their story via the story of the Al Haddad family, which happened a few hours later and had a much more tragic end.

Majda, who is a poet with her own website, but also the pretty and youthful looking mum of Tala (7), Dima (12), Firas (13), Basher (14), and Mohanned (16), told me the area their building was in was targeted from about 1am that night. They hid in their middle room, away from any outside walls. Early on they thought maybe it was specifically their building being targeted with rockets and about to be destroyed, so they ran into the street, but then decided it was the nextdoor building and that the street was even more dangerous because the Israeli planes were shooting anything that moved.

So they spent the night awake and frightened, praying, thinking they would never see daylight. At 6am three phosphorus shells hit their building, setting their cousin's ground floor flat on fire, and they realised some of the buildings near them were on fire too. The phosphorus fumes made it almost impossible to breath, and then at 7.30am an F16 plane dropped a missile on the main road beside them (I saw the enormous crater) and the exploding rubble smashed all their windows and doors. Terrified, they fled the building again.

Majda's husband Nasser and Basher and Firas attempted to get their car, but it wouldn't start. Majda and Mohanned tried to get the girls away across the street. They got as far as the wall beside the street, and a tank – that could clearly see they were a family group carrying small bags – opened fire on them as they cowered against the wall. Mohanned made it across the street, but Majda dropped the bags and tried to shield the girls. 'Mohanned was calling something to me but the attack was so loud I couldn't hear. I tried to run to him with the girls, but fell on the street. I was injured and bleeding but I crawled over to him.'

By this time Majda couldn't see where her husband or other sons were, and the mobile wouldn't work. When she finally got through for a moment, her husband told her he and Basher had been shot, were unable to move, and were lying flat on the street in the hope of surviving the combined land and air attack, in sight of the tanks that had already shot them. Getting her other three children to shelter, Majda tried to call the ambulance, the Red Cross, even a radio station, but the phone wouldn't work. So she set out to run to Al Shifa hospital for help.

When she said this, I stopped to check I'd understood. Al Quds hospital is five minutes away and Al Shifa is at least a kilometre, it takes me about half an hour to walk there from Al Quds. Majda explained that she knew from the radio that Al Quds was under the same attack as they were and there was no way she could make it there alive, nor could anyone there reach them alive, which was in fact true.

In the meantime, 13 year old Firas was also going for help for his brother and father, but almost immediately he was shot in the knee by an Israeli sniper. This didn't stop him however – he covered at least 60 yards, half of them in sight of the tanks, to reach his cousin's house. His cousin managed to contact a neighbour who was a doctor with a UN car, and they went into the line of fire and picked up Nasser and Basher and got them to Al Shifa. By the time Majda reached Al Shifa (I still can't get my head around how she must have felt during that run) her husband was in surgery and her son was also being treated.

Now, she has her two boys safe in her own double bed, each with a bandaged leg. Basher has steel bolts in his – he lost a large chunk of the lower leg to what was described to me as a large bullet. He was due to enter a kung fu championship, so that's had to be put on hold, but he was apparently bravely joking with his nurse, during a painful dressing change, that he could still kick with the other leg.

Firas is going to have an operation on Tuesday because his knee needs putting back together, to what extent it can be. Mohammed and Hazem, volunteer nurses-in-training attached to Al Shifa, come in daily to care for them. Both boys have lovely smiles, and their mother says they mostly behave well to each other while sharing the bed. Their father Nasser, an engineer with no work for more than two years as the siege allows few building materials in, is still in Egypt being treated. As I understand it, his hip, kidney and prostate are all damaged.

Dima and Tala come in from school while I am there, being treated to the usual coffee and Arabic sweets. Such small girls. 'Are *they* terrorists?' asks their mother. 'My family cares about all people. We don't mind if they are from a different country or a different religion. We think all people are the same. That's what we believe.'

FEBRUARY 2

I'm told the bursts of noise that are currently shaking the internet cafe a little are probably F16 sonic booms and not rockets, so that's nice! Last night's attacks involved seven rockets on the tunnel/border area of Rafah and a strike on an empty police station in Gaza City.

Al Jazeera English reported:

> The military said Sunday's attacks were the beginning of a new wave of raids over Gaza, but did not elaborate... Ehud Olmert, Israel's out-going prime minister, said that the military would respond to attacks in a 'severe and disproportionate' fashion after at least 10 rockets and mortar shells hit southern Israel on Sunday... The al-Aqsa Martyrs Brigades, the military wing of the Fatah faction led by Mahmoud Abbas, the Palestinian president, told Al Jazeera that it carried out the attacks.[2]

Israel bills the attacks as a 'response' to rockets (note it's not Hamas rockets this time; the armed resistance in Gaza is cross political, Hamas does not actually control it all). I guess my thoughts on this will be obvious.

I have just come from Al Shifa hospital, where we were helping with the paperwork of four children with attack injuries such as internal bleeding, or kidney transplant requirements, who we hope are going to be sent out to France for treatment. Amira (who I wrote about on January 26), who lost all her family, is one of them. She has both internal injuries and similar bolts in her crushed leg to Basher in the Nadeem family. She can still find a smile except when dealing with the pain of injections. Two women with injured babies, one with

'Disproportionate responses' and armed resistance

Supporters of both Palestine and Israel invoke international law in support of their side. Israel has repeatedly claimed that it launched Operation Cast Lead in response to rocket attacks by Hamas and other Palestinian fighters which have hit southern Israeli towns such as Sderot. Supporters of Palestine have countered that Israeli armed responses have been out of all proportion to Palestinian strength or the extent of Palestinian militants' action. The comment of Israeli Prime Minister Ehud Olmert that Palestinian rocket fire would bring a 'severe and disproportionate response' confirms this to many.

Physicians For Human Rights commented on the claim of Israel's self-defence and the proportionality of Israeli responses:

> International law requires that the use of force comply with Article 51 of the Charter of the UN: it must be invoked in response to an 'armed attack' and be 'necessary and proportionate', otherwise it amounts to an aggression... the International Court of Justice (ICJ) clearly stipulates that a self defence intervention should comply with the laws of armed conflict. In the Nicaragua vs. USA case of 1986, the ICJ establishes a hierarchy in the gravity of threats and attacks. In the present case, it is questionable whether an occupying power can invoke self-defence against its own occupied territories.

On the issue of the right of resistance to occupation, UN General Assembly resolution 2105 XX of December 1965 states that the UN 'recognises the legitimacy of the struggles by the people under colonial rule to exercise their right to self-determination and independence and invites all States to provide material and moral assistance to the national liberation movements in colonial Territories'. The 1977 Protocols, an addition to the 1949 Geneva Convention, further elaborated on the legitimacy of 'armed conflicts in which peoples are fighting against colonial domination and alien occupation and against racist regimes in the exercise of their right of self determination'.

Other legal arguments put forward in support of Palestinian right to resistance centre on Israel's failure to observe the many UN General Assembly and Security Council resolutions which have been passed since 1948 demanding

▶

that it respect Palestinian rights such as the right of return or compensation for refugees, withdrawal from territory occupied in 1967 and 1973, and the right to self-determination for both parties.

As Richard Falk, now UN Special Rapporteur for Human Rights in the Occupied Territories, put it in 2000: 'Israel's failures to abide by international law, as a belligerent occupant, amounted to a fundamental denial of the right of self-determination, and more generally of respect for the framework of belligerent occupation – giving rise to a Palestinian right of resistance.'

References: Physicians for Human Rights, 'Independent fact-finding mission into violations of human rights in the Gaza Strip during the period 27.12.2008 – 18.01.2009', April 2009; *Telegraph*, 'Israel vows "disproportionate" response to Gaza rocket attacks', February 1, 2009; Richard Falk, 'International Law and the al-Aqsa Intifada', Middle East Report 217, Winter 2000; US Army International & Operational Law Department, *Laws of War Handbook*, 2004.

phosphorus burns over half his body and I think the other also with burns, share her room, and Amira's aunt and the other women visitors have formed the usual atmosphere of community, with shared food and support for each other.

A few days ago Ewa and I went to visit Hassan in Khan Younis. He was the Jabalia medic who Eva and Alberto filmed being shot by a sniper. Israeli Physicians for Human Rights are quoting the WHO's statement that 16 emergency workers were killed in the recent attacks and 25 were wounded. In fact we understand the wounded figure may now have reached nearly 40.

After Hassan met us, we dropped by to visit the Khan Younis Red Crescent base – I'd not been there before – and of course had to stop for tea and a chat. The Khan Younis Red Crescent hosted British filmmaker James Miller for ten days, before he was shot dead here by Israel in 2003. We met Halil Al Subba, who had his own war wounds from going on a call to Khoza'a during a white phosphorus strike there. This in itself was extremely courageous as Israel had declared it a closed military zone and was giving no permission for the wounded to be collected or anyone to be evacuated.

All Halil remembers is getting out of the driving seat into thick smoke; he passed out instantly as the masks the medics had were of no use against phosphorus. His colleagues got him back to the hospital. He was unconscious for three hours, but appeared recovered enough to be sent home after some basic treatment. However when he found he had pain that felt like a knife in his chest, he went back to the hospital where X-rays showed severe internal burns to his lungs.

A Greek medical delegation said they have never seen anything like his injuries, and other medical people have speculated that the phosphorus is mixed with other unidentified chemicals. One of the current problems is that doctors can't clearly know how to treat injuries when they don't clearly know the causes. Halil has had antibiotics. But no-one knows what long-term effects he may expect. When he found out I work with ISM, he told me that he was one of the medics who brought in Rachel Corrie after she was run over by an Israeli bulldozer in 2003.

We were fed a wonderful lunch at Hassan's family home, meeting his lovely wife, children Fawzi, Annan (his little girl who is named after Kofi Annan) and baby Ali, and his extended family. We also got to see the stove Hassan invented, which he was self-deprecatingly telling us about on a Jabalia ambulance shift when I first met him. Not that I really understand, but it involves an old fridge fuel tank in which he can compress the air using a bike pump, turning the fuel from a liquid into a gas, which then burns much more efficiently for cooking use. Ewa and I were extremely impressed. We don't have any cooking gas at home either, but we just complain about it!

6
FEBRUARY 3–MARCH 19, 2009

Farming Under Fire

FEBRUARY 3

It is not only fishermen that Israel regularly shoots, but farmers also, and they too say it's got worse since the ceasefire. Last week, 27 year old Anwar Il Ibrim was killed while harvesting parsley, just down the road from our friends in Al Faraheen. The other farmers at Abassan Jadida, near Khan Younis, have asked for accompaniment in the continuing quest to bring home the parsley, today from a field that supports 15 families. We had an Italian film crew along as well, Indymedia types at heart, but documenting the war for mainstream TV.

We had two quiet hours in the bright sun. I stood reading. Stelios, more responsible, didn't leave off scanning the other side of the border fence; he and Andrew were in charge of the ISM filming. The young farmers bent, cutting green swathes and bundling them into one-shekel bunches for later loading on the cart. Ewa joined in, until they kindly told her she was rubbish at it. Closer to the border fence, a donkey grazed – in danger, but because of the siege there is not enough animal feed for there to be any alternative.

'Got any chocolate?' I texted Vik, who stood in the distance, wearing the cream dinner jacket he'd borrowed against the winter cold and not taken off all war. It went rather fetchingly with his combat boots.

147

'I have only *prezzomolo*,' he sent back. I looked up hopefully; this sounded like an Italian delicacy. But he shook his head, and pointed at the green sea in which we stood. Oh. That'll be Italian for parsley, then. I tried a mouthful. It was rather nice.

At about 1pm, inevitably, the Israeli soldiers arrived in their jeeps on the other side of the fence. There was a pause, and then a loud crack. The shooting had begun – the farmers dropped to the ground. Because she was beside them, so did Ewa, but was on her feet again in seconds as will overcame instinct. The film crew continued to film from ground level. The shots seemed loud but I found it hard to judge how close they were. Were these warning shots?

Hands in the air, fluorescent vests shared out, we eyed the soldiers. Over the megaphone we stated the obvious. 'Please stop shooting. We are unarmed civilians. We are international observers. We are harvesting parsley. We are no threat. A television crew is filming your actions. Please stop shooting.' They didn't.

We called West Bank ISM. The farmers decided to alternate lying in the ditches during firing, with leaping up and picking parsley at top speed during the quieter moments. But the shots moved steadily closer.

Eva shook her head in disbelief. 'If I can see the jeeps, the soldiers' shapes and uniforms, then they can see our yellow vests, our cameras, our donkey carts, our empty hands,' she said. We checked with the farmers; they'd had enough. Two wagonloads of parsley would have to do.

'We are finished for the day. We are leaving. Please stop shooting,' we announced. It is quite hard to turn your back on bullets, and now they were very close, whizzing past our ears, hitting the dirt around us, and directed to ricochet off the destroyed home we were passing. As soon as they were behind the building, the farmers began to run.

Our West Bank support had called our embassies; the Canadian embassy called Eva back. 'We're told you are being shot at.' It seemed to take a little while before it dawned on the person on the phone that the shooting was coming from the Israeli side. 'How do you know it was *Israeli* soldiers shooting at you?' she asked. Did she really think it was more likely that *Palestinians* would be shooting at Palestinian farmers and their human rights accompaniers, than that Israeli soldiers would be? Israel sure does have a good PR machine. Polite as always, Eva explained that given the Israeli jeeps, the Israeli soldiers, and the Israeli guns all located at the point from which the bullets originated, it was a safe bet.

FEBRUARY 5

Today was like a repeat of two days ago: same field, same parsley, same farmers, same shooting from Israeli soldiers, yet this time only half an hour of work was completed before bullets flew. Yousef from Press TV had advised us to film an interview under fire; thanks Yousef. Stelios held the camera, I peered out from under my funny hat, hands in the air, attempting to say all the right things, as everyone behind me tried to resist their 'duck' reflex. Shouldn't this be enough to make prime time TV? Somewhere?

Before the war began, Israel broke the irrigation pipes, and the plants become increasingly tough and inedible without water. If they are not harvested now, all the resources that went into their planting – itself a death-defying exercise – will be wasted.

Anwar, who died harvesting, hadn't worked in this area for six months, since Israel's May 2008 incursion had heightened the danger, his mother told us. But he was the only son, and his father needed medicine.

The owner of the land, Yusuf Abu Shaheen, commented after Tuesday's gun-fire, 'If you hadn't been with us today, the soldiers would have killed us all.'

FEBRUARY 6

On January 31 I wrote about the Nadeems who tried to escape from Israel's attacks on Tel al Howa in their car, but it wouldn't start. Also on January 15, an hour or so afterwards at about 10.15am, their neighbours the Al Haddads tried to escape in their car.

They only got a few yards.

The Kabariti family told me about this, because Mahfouz's sister's family are also neighbours to the Al Haddads. Mahfouz took me to hear the story from Mazin, brother to Adi Al Haddad.

The Al Haddad family, in the same terror of remaining in their building to die that the Nadeems described, decided the safest way to leave was in their car. Believing they were about to lose everything, they took with them a large sum of money, the price of some family land that had just been sold. Adi, with his wife Ahsan, about 40, son Hatam, aged 20, daughter Ala'a, aged 14, and Mohammed aged 23, drove from their sidestreet into their normally quiet road. To their right, a few hundred yards away, were the tanks that had targeted the Nadeems. To their left, also a few hundred yards away, the main road that had already been hit by F16 planes.

They got to where their road and the main road intersect. At this point the Israeli army struck the car from both tank and plane, apparently with two rockets or shells, and at least one phosphorus bomb. The car spun 15 metres away, and as one of the doors flew open, Mohammed was thrown out, catching only the initial brunt of the phosphorus before the car exploded. Abu Rami il Sharif, who lived in the same block as the Haddads and on the corner of this intersection, was able to reach him. As firing continued from the tanks, Abu Rami knew that he could not reach the car to help anyone else, but he knew also that there was no-one left to help.

Helmi Abu Shaban, living opposite Abu Rami on the other side of the street, ventured out to the car at midday. The phosphorus fire was still burning, and looking inside the car, he could see nothing to show any humans had ever been there. Not even any bones. Just ashes.

I went to see Mohammed in Al Shifa hospital last week. When I got there, Ramattan TV was waiting to interview him, and I couldn't bring myself to ask him to tell the story to me also. I just told him quietly that I was sorry, and left. He has lost an eye and has burns all down one side of his body. I understand he has only a little brother left, who wasn't with the family at the time.

FEBRUARY 8

Before the strikes, 14 Friends of Palestine, a group in Marin County, California, asked Eva and me to make contact with a little girl, Khitam, whom they sponsor via Atfaluna Society for Deaf Children. It's taken a while for us to follow this up, but we got there today. We followed our usual pattern; meeting at Al Shifa hospital, grabbing a *falafel* sandwich, then striding off down the dusty streets ignoring all the beeping taxis (shared taxis are as close as Gaza gets to public transport).

Twenty minutes later, I am startled by the wholeness of the Atfaluna building. Several of the buildings nearby are in small concrete pieces, but Atfaluna has grass, and windows. I doubt Israel avoided Atfaluna deliberately, since they bombed schools and hospitals, so Atfaluna also has good luck. Inside, we meet Suad, who has arranged for Khitam's social worker Mariam to take us to visit her family. They live in Shuja'iyya, in four rooms – Khitam's parents, and their seven girls (born in a row), followed by four boys, the last one a smiley 5 months.

Khitam's mum is a friendly woman, who tries to coax her girls, just home from school, to appear in anything other than shyly giggling glimpses, though we do eventually manage a photo with some of them. She manages to introduce us to two of the little boys with the lure of the Arabic sweets we'd brought. We ask her how the Israeli strikes had affected them; she says they stayed in their home for the first ten days but the rocket attacks then became too close and frightening and they moved in with their downstairs neighbours, the only place they had to go.

The bread shortage has hit them hard, she says, describing bargaining for a bag of flour and being 20 shekels (about £3) short. A wave of guilt hits me; if only we had got to them before the attacks, they would have had the equivalent of Khitam's dad's salary for a month (he's a cleaner). Khitam's mum, apparently not giving this a moment's thought, cheerfully says they did manage to get the flour in the end. The bread shortage continues, and the money is just as welcome now.

Khitam's home is very simple, they don't have much, and when we ask her mum what the donation might go on, it's clear they will carefully keep themselves in the basics for the children to be well and comfortable: mattresses, floor mats, food, clothes, gas maybe.

Eva heads off to see if 18 year old Abd at Al Wafa is managing to imagine some sort of life for himself in a wheelchair yet. Back at Atfaluna, I am taken to meet Khitam herself, in amongst a class full of beaming kids. She leaps from her chair, glowing at finding herself the centre of attention. Mariam signs to her that we come representing 14 Friends of Palestine, and have met her family. She introduces herself to me with her sign name, a curving stroke of her finger from her forehead to her cheek, imitating the sweep of her dark curly hair. I am pleased to be able to return the sign name I was given once, placing an imaginary hat on my head (I like hats).

Then I am taken down to the kindergarten class, in a series of green carpeted rooms that imitate a lush outdoors that Gaza City children don't see, except here where there are also gardens outside. They also bubble over with enthusiasm for a visitor, and I learn the Palestinian sign for *salaam aleikum*. Surrounded by energetic and joyful small people, I realise what incredibly expressive faces and bodies deaf children can develop, with space and permission to move from supportive teachers, many of whom are deaf themselves. Next I go to see some of the traditional craftwork the adults who work here produce.

This place is amazing. For the first time ever, I am seeing what Palestinians look like when they are surrounded by beauty: by art, by books and resources, by unbroken, unbombed, undamaged, *working* things. It makes me want to cry. (Currently a lot of random stuff makes me want to cry; I didn't cry for any of those broken, bombed, damaged children in my ambulance and I guess that sadness is waiting somewhere deep.)

300 children are studying at Atfaluna. 150 are on the waiting list. While the building continues to stay in one piece, they will grow up with a vision that hearing Gaza children will simply have to imagine; what the world looks like when it isn't all dust and crumbled concrete.

FEBRUARY 10

On Tuesday night I went to smoke *shisha* and eat cake with the Red Crescent volunteers for Musa's 29th birthday. There were the usual accusative cries of '*wen inti?*' – where have you been? These folks got used to me being round the hospital 24 hours; Palestinians tend to start missing you about an hour after you left them, and if a week passes without a visit their feelings are quite hurt. The frequent cracks of thunder outside the cafe made us all smile – just because they weren't rockets or shells. 'No attack – but still *shisha*!' said Saleh happily, referring to all the times I'd spent with them, smoking in the smashed-up buildings as explosions rocked us.

I am so glad they are all alive. I tell them that when I come back here after my degree, in three years' time, they will all be married with children. Beautiful young nurse Raja is sitting next to me; I tell her about where I was today when this thunderstorm began. We'd had a quiet morning parsley picking in Faraheen, with no shooting, but as we were travelling back we had a call from Beit Hanoun, asking us to come and be an international presence for a search for a *shaheed*. So ISM West Bank contacted the army in advance and got a verbal assurance from the DCO that as long as we were unarmed (I'll leave my M16 at home then...) they would not shoot. It was unusual for this kind of contact to be made, and I think this was the only time it happened: by law the onus is on the army not to shoot civilians, not upon Palestinians, or us, to prove we are not legitimate targets.

This *shaheed* was a 21 year old resistance fighter; his neighbourhood knew he had recently been shot from an Apache near the border, but they couldn't find his body. About 100 men and women, including the Red Crescent, had been looking all day, except for in an area right beside the barbed wire fence, below some Israeli watchtowers, which they felt was too dangerous to go near, so they saved it for us. We found ourselves walking past empty, flattened houses, past shepherds grazing their sheep, into the empty land beside the border.

As we walked, the sky darkened increasingly and rain began to pelt down, creating a strangely apocalyptic atmosphere. Tension heightened amongst the people we were with, who began hurriedly to search the uneven ground. The internationals split into groups to accompany them; Eva and I went to walk the stretch beside the barbed wire border in our fluorescent vests, persuading the young men to stay further away, for our own safety as well as theirs. I've never been this close to the border. An Israeli jeep loomed above us, and we stopped so I could call out to its occupants that we were here to look for a body and then we would leave.

The wind was howling, and I wondered if they could hear us. As I was wondering this, there was a shout – the body of the young man had been found. At the same time a warning shot was fired. Hands in the air we backed away from the border towards the group gathered around the body, trying to ease it onto a makeshift stretcher. An Israeli soldier began repeatedly to announce something unintelligible, and we called back – 'we can't hear you'.

Then suddenly I could hear better (it was the usual 'closed military zone – leave right now or we will open fire') and turning round, I realised two of the soldiers had walked out of their shelter and come down nearer to the fence to call out, demonstrating an understanding that we were no threat to them. It was a strange moment, because it felt like they might just have made that extra effort to establish communication. Ewa says she also heard them say 'what are you doing?', so the DCO's official notification didn't seem to have got far.

Several of our group took turns with the megaphone, Ewa is particularly good at being polite: 'Please don't shoot! We're just collecting this body and we'll be leaving. Please don't shoot!' Then we followed the Beit Hanoun folks carrying the body through the mud, past the broken houses, to the waiting Red Crescent ambulance. It seemed a long way. I was expecting the crack of gunfire at every step. But it never came. Later, as we left the Beit Hanoun hospital, I caught a glimpse of a young boy's face, crumpled into tears. A younger brother, maybe.

In response to this story, Raja tells me about her brother, who was 19 when he died, having joined the Palestinian resistance with his two best friends, from whom he had always been inseparable. They died together as the result of an informer's tip-off.

FEBRUARY 11

Last night after Musa's birthday party, I walked round the corner from Al Quds hospital complex with him to the re-occupied 101 Ambulance Dispatch Centre. (I suffered a momentary sense of homelessness when I went to Al Quds the other day and discovered the temporary dispatch room had returned to its former office identity and the '101' sign was gone from the door.)

The regular Dispatch Centre is in the Red Crescent complex that they had to evacuate after the initial December 27 attacks, because of an unexploded rocket in it. It also includes a storage and distribution centre, and the ambulance park-up, which is burned and blackened, as are some of the ambulances.

6.1 The Red Crescent ambulance compound in Tel al Howa, around the corner from Al Quds hospital, was destroyed during the early days of attacks, along with several ambulances.

Sharyn Lock

I didn't know, during those crazy days in Al Quds, that Ahmed, a friend of mine we'd lost touch with, actually was hiding very close to me in his family house there. Like Reem (who is doing ok in her business studies exams this week), they were in the line of the tanks and didn't dare move.

When I finally saw him last week, and my colleague Natalie who stays with university professor Dr Asad's family opposite the Red Crescent complex, they told me that the houses in the area had again received the recorded phone calls Israel sends to Gaza people, with the same instructions used during the January attacks: 'Your houses will be destroyed – move away from them and go to the city centre.' I'd always thought Tel al Howa counted as the city centre. They and many others resignedly stayed home, though I imagine some families exhaustedly packed up again and vacated for a while. Nothing happened in their area, though shelling was occurring in Rafah around that time.

On January 19, the day after the 'ceasefire', I finally walked around this area, and understood just why everyone living in apartment buildings in this area ran to Al Quds hospital… I cannot see a single residential building that remains whole.

FEBRUARY 16

A South African teacher who reads my blog asked yesterday: 'I've heard that everyday people are still being killed in Gaza, is this true?'

Yes. Almost every day there are further injuries, and often deaths. And as usual, most of the time they are civilians. On Saturday February 14, I was talking to medic friends on duty at Al Quds hospital, and they broke off the conversation to run to their ambulance; I just caught the words '*al mina*' – the port. Two ISMers went later to interview the fishermen who had come under attack from Israeli gunboats at three miles out. The injured fisherman, Rafik Abu Rayala, had shrapnel in his back which had resulted in internal bleeding. His boat is a *hassaka*, small and wooden, powered only by an outboard motor.

Two days ago six people were injured in an attack on Beach camp from gunboats at sea. Some of us today visited one of them in Shifa hospital: Ali, 19, was walking with his friend on the beach. They saw the first rocket coming, ran, and escaped it. The second one got them. Ali has lost one hand and three fingers on the other hand. One of his eyes was saved despite damage, the other was destroyed and the wound is currently infected. Multiple pieces of shrapnel have wounded his face and other areas of his body.

Farmers and fishermen fear attacks every day, but what choice do they have? The fish and the cropland are where they are; it's the Gaza sea and Gaza land, but this seems to make no difference to Israel. We've been accompanying farm workers in Abassan Jadida, Al Faraheen, for seven days now I think, and on four of them, including yesterday, we were all shot at.

6.2   Caoimhe remains visible in the Red Crescent vest as the farmers pick parsley under sporadic gunfire from the Israeli border on February 12. Six days later, one of them was shot in the foot.

Sharyn Lock

What can be seen clearly from some of Stelios and Andrew's film footage (which we put on the internet) is how clearly unthreatened the soldiers feel by our presence, in terms of their own safety. Six or seven of them were visible to us between the episodes of shooting, as they wandered about between the jeeps and the tank. And that day they actually left us alone until we finished our first field, not shooting until we'd moved to the second field, which was in fact a little further away from the border than the first one. There is no logic to any of this.

On one of the days we were there, February 7, we went to the beanfield next to where Anwar was killed. The men had started early in the hope the army wouldn't be out to shoot at them yet, but still the shooting had started before we arrived at 8am. So then the women went out instead, but they were pretty scared, and only decided to continue because we were there. Work finished without further shooting.

Yesterday, February 15, we had a small victory. Three jeeps and a tank delivered soldiers who shot at us for a while, not as close or as enthusiastically as other days, but ignoring any bullets in your vicinity still requires courage. The farmers stayed on the land. After a bit the jeeps and the tank left, and the farmers worked until they were done for the day.

After that we went to visit our friends Sobhe and Yara in their temporary village centre house. They insisted on feeding us a lovely lunch, mostly from their own hard-won produce, before we accompanied them to their regular house and land on the edge of Al Faraheen, facing the border. They don't feel it's safe enough to live in now because they are often shot at there. Yesterday Sobhe had asked for our presence and help while he sprayed his onion crop and harvested radishes. We realised the village we could see from his fields was Khoza'a, hit so hard during the war. Was it being beside the Israeli border they were being punished for too?

The same day we were with the women as they picked beans, Al Faraheen folks were proud to show us the communal bakery they've recently built, opened for its first day of operation. For one shekel (about 20p), you can bake ten pieces of bread that you've made at home. This is a communal response to the gas shortage that makes it so hard for individual families to keep themselves in bread.

This afternoon, we went out to Beit Hanoun to be an international presence to assist some farmers moving their bee hives, as they too are now in an area considered too dangerous to visit regularly. Inevitably: more shooting.

Language and time limitations mean I can't always record all the injuries and deaths still occurring here as a result of continued Israeli attacks. Often we hear explosions, and it will take a day or two before we find out accurately what they were and who they affected. This week I am going to resume a regular weekly ambulance shift so that I can keep some level of awareness and witnessing.

FEBRUARY 18

One of our farmers was shot in the foot today. As Murphy's law would have it, this was actually the first day I didn't go farming, technically leaving the group without a medic, but I sent my medic kit with the ISMers and one of them did some impromptu foot bandaging for 20 year old Mohammed, who was loading spinach ready to leave at the time he was shot. Faraheen farmers will go out again to harvest on Saturday and have asked us to join them. Food is not optional.

Israel permitted a shipment of cooking gas today, after a two week embargo. Gaza consumes 350 tonnes a day. About two weeks ago, I was present when John Ging of UNRWA told a legal delegation from the USA about the amount of aid that was being allowed through to Gaza. He explained that UNRWA is responsible for feeding 900,000 people with refugee status (Gaza has at least 50 per cent unemployment). Yet only enough of UNRWA's supply trucks are being let through to feed 30,000 of them. He said they were lucky if they got 100 trucks a day currently. *Less* than in December 2008, before the attacks. At which point, due to the ongoing siege, UNRWA's food supplies had in fact been drained totally. Yet the border has the capacity to process 14,000 trucks a day. Bottom line: Israel wants to starve people. What other conclusion can be drawn?

I was off farming duty today because I spent last night on ambulance duty, with medic Gamal. He was telling me that he'd not only had to collect shot fisherman Rafik on Valentine's Day, but also a 15 year old from Shuja'iyya, killed by a shot to the head, near Al Wafa hospital. On January 27 I described the constant Israeli shooting we heard when we went there, and the hospital staff telling us that this was normal.

Our main incident from the night was a top speed delivery of visiting Moroccan doctors from Al Quds hospital to Rafah hospital, to provide surgery to a child of about 12 who had multiple abdomen perforations, apparently from a previously unexploded bomb.

In the last days I was in touch with two people I knew through the Union of Health Work Committees Gaza head office, where I was volunteering before the attacks. Basma I've seen a few times now, I went and visited her family in Beit Hanoun after bee-moving the other day. I lost contact with her during the attacks due to the phones not working, so I was very pleased to see her. In answer to my enquiries, she said her family and house were fine. But a short while later she quietly mentioned that a cousin and her child had been killed.

Then when we met again, she told me what I should have noticed myself the first time – that she'd lost all her front teeth. She fell and smashed them while her family were running away from the attacks on their home. I hate to think how long it took before she got any dental care or even pain relief.

I bumped into the manager of Al Asria Children's Centre today. He was the same smiling, friendly man I originally met in December. I asked him how many children he had, and he told me of his five daughters. Then he mentioned that he also now had a son. A baby of 2 months, his brother's boy, who is now his responsibility to care for, because his brother was killed in the attacks when the baby was 36 days old. The baby's mother survives also, a widow after a little over a year of marriage.

At one ambulance home visit last night, medic Gamal and co-worker Mohammed *and* their patient were all puffing away on cigarettes, which makes someone like me, from the smoke-free land of the UK, smile wryly (I can't talk, given the frequency with which I mention *shisha* sessions). But I can understand much better now how hard it is to worry about lung cancer, in a place like this. So many people just don't live that long. Or if they do, it's without an eye, or a hand, or legs. And who knows what the phosphorus did to everyone's lungs anyway.

Environmental issues are the same. Ecological campaigning was my first love, and I continue to bewilder shopkeepers here by fighting off the offers of plastic bags. But it's even more of a token gesture than normal. Gazan daily life depends on cheap and replaceable plastic. I hate the stuff. I hate disposable everything. But here anything else is a luxury for almost everyone, and probably isn't available anyway. And the rubbish that blows about still, from the weeks of war when it couldn't be collected, just seems so beside the point.

No-one who knows me will believe this, but with the ambulances, during the attacks, I so lost my sense of any future beyond the moment, that I too began to do what most of the medics did due to lack of time and facilities… I would peel off bloodied plastic gloves and simply drop them on the ground. Now I see these gloves fluttering about still, maybe marking a spot where a limb, or a life, was saved or lost. All over Gaza.

FEBRUARY 19

When Israeli soldiers shot 20 year old deaf farmer Mohammad al-Buraim in the leg yesterday, the bullet went straight through his ankle and landed in the tyre of the parsley-loaded truck he'd been pushing. Mohammed supports a family of 16.

The Israeli Hummer vehicle had sat observing for 30 minutes before the soldiers opened fire, and the initial bullets were so close the farmers told the five human rights observers present that they would immediately pack up and leave. The soldiers continued to shoot after Mohammed was injured, with bullets whizzing past every few seconds.

Eva later wrote down the farmers' version of events. Yasser Rizek Samoud, also 20, was next to Mohammed when the Israeli soldiers began shooting. He told her:

> We had stopped our work and were ready to leave. The pickup truck wasn't starting, so we were pushing it. The Israeli soldiers started shooting at us from the border area. Mohammed was hit in the leg. I carried him about 2 metres before they started shooting again. We were able to get him to a truck on the road, which took him towards the town. An ambulance picked him up from the truck and took him to Nasser hospital in Khan Younis.

Israel bans entry of seeds, fertilisers, and machinery replacement parts into Gaza. Shooting the farmers as well seems just gratuitous really.

Eva writes on her blog:

> From his hospital bed, charismatic and likeable Mohammed al-Buraim assures us that he'll be okay, even after the assault. But no way will he go near the field. 'You think I'm crazy?!' he signs.
>
> Mohammed marks the fourth shooting of Palestinians in the 'buffer zone' in the last few weeks. The three shootings prior to Mohammed's were: on 18 January, Maher Abu-Rajileh (24), from Huza'ah village, east of Khan Younis, was killed by IOF soldiers while working on his land 400m from the Green Line; on 20 January, at 1 pm, Israeli soldiers shot Waleed al-Astal (42) of Al Qarara, near Khan Younis, in his right foot; and on 27 January, Anwar al-Buraim was shot in the neck and killed.

Anwar was Mohammed's cousin.

FEBRUARY 23

Today is the second day I have gone to spend the hour before sunset on a small pier that juts into the waves of the silver Gaza sea. Small lights bob from fishing boats courageous or desperate enough to brave the gunboats. To my right is the crumbled concrete of the port. To my left and behind is the crumpled concrete of the government buildings whose destruction made my apartment shake on December 27. I turn up Ani Di Franco's *Swan Dive* very loud.

Everyone was talking today about the deafening noise of the F16s flying low over us this morning, in Rafah as well as here, so maybe all over Gaza. Netanyahu saying hello, people were joking.[1] Angela from the Israeli Committee Against House Demolitions was texting me yesterday to recommend black humour as an antidote to self-pity. It occurred to me that I don't know how to tell the difference between self-pity and healthy sadness. I tend to suspect most forms of sadness or depression of being self-pity. It's impossible to feel any kind of sadness yourself here without thinking of the thousands of bereaved parents and children, and how irrelevant and self-indulgent your own emotions are. Of course that doesn't make you feel better, just guilty.

I can't even feel sad with a clear focus. Ask me what I'm feeling sad about, I'll not be able to tell you anything in particular. It's a real and incapacitating feeling, because it makes it hard to do anything but creep back into bed where you can pretend nothing can get you (except F16s and tanks, which got many people in their beds in January). But it's missing its subject. Am I feeling sad about the aforementioned dead children? Specifically the ones in my ambulance? Probably. At a guess.

Give me content to concentrate on, and immediately there is an accessible feeling: not sadness, but horror. If I think of the realities of life here, I just can't get past blank horror. There is a picture of a baby doing the rounds (the video clip keeps being taken down) that was first burned and then had its legs chewed off by dogs – perhaps the same IOF dogs that attacked a bedridden 100 year old man during an incursion into the West Bank this week?[2] The ambulance men holding the baby are two of our friends from Jabalia Red Crescent. What kind of dreams do they have at night?

What do we do? I don't know. People on the outside think I'm doing something, but right now, I'm not. I'm stuck in the fallout of January, and I'm not particularly useful. I know my blog readers don't mind. I know even my donors don't mind. I know just continuing to be an international in the area, when attacks might start again anytime – what am I saying? they haven't stopped – might *increase* anytime – is enough. I know I am getting the occasional useful report written, and I am making locals happy by drinking tea with them, which says nothing about me and everything about how much Palestinians delight in visitors.

I know people will email and say it's ok, and that I sound like I maybe have post traumatic stress disorder. I think I've had that for years, I probably wouldn't know where I was without it. And alongside 1.5 million people who probably have had it for years too, I feel at home. But we're still shouting at each other and crying for none of the real reasons and then reverting to blank, numb horror.

And we're still going out farming tomorrow, in Khoza'a this time, which we heard had a visit from Israeli tanks last Friday. On Wednesday, six of my group are beginning First Responder medic training in the Palestinian Red Crescent Training Institute in Khan Younis, three days a week. At the institute they have one of those training dummies you practise resuscitation on. His limbs move bonelessly, you can fold his legs back on themselves and pack him into a suitcase. Ewa and I looked at him, then at each other, thinking the same two things: (1) We seem to be doing this the wrong way round, starting with real people and moving onto pretend people. (2) We had real people in our ambulances whose legs did that.

I am trying to do the right things. I am listening to music, and playing guitar, and today we went to dance *dubke* (I spent the whole class feeling extremely angry about the steps I couldn't get – see what I mean about all the emotions being in the wrong place!) and tomorrow Eva and I might manage to set ourselves up a *tai kwon do* class, which I think could either be a very good thing or a very bad thing, we will see. It could burn off some of what I'm feeling; on the other hand, feeling angry and being able to punch well may not be the best combination. And I smoke *shisha* every day because I can always blame the phosphorus gas for cancer now, and it brings me the small amount of peace that I am very hungry for, but which can't be found anywhere in this broken place.

There go those F16s again, frightening a thousand small children awake.

FEBRUARY 24

In Khoza'a today the farmers requesting our accompaniment were mostly elderly and mostly women, and the bullets were so close they could only face five minutes of them. You could feel the thud of the air on your body as they flew past, they made our ears ring, and the shooting continued for about 20 minutes as we all walked away – one bullet hit a tree beside us.

I feel so worn down by this insanity at the moment, that the bullets today really shook me – I could easily imagine the next one slamming into my head – giving me a tiny glimpse into life as a farmer here.

Then, some hours after we left, they shot a teenage girl in the leg.

FEBRUARY 25

Today we went to see 17 year old Wafa Al Najar, who was shot yesterday, in Nasser hospital in Khan Younis. In Palestinian tradition, both her family and neighbours were keeping her company. But they were able to do little for her, and while they all at once told us the story of her shooting and of Khoza'a, their village (where Israel has been accused of war crimes in the recent attacks),[3] Wafa sobbed intermittently in pain.

During the recent attacks, somewhere between December 27–30, Wafa's 20 year old brother, Jihad Ahmad Al Najar, died in a Cairo hospital, evacuated there after he was shot in the head. Then, like thousands near the border, her family's Khoza'a home was one of 163 locally destroyed by the Israeli army. (The army also bulldozed 1,500 *dunums*, about 150 hectares, of farmland there.) Yesterday at about 4pm, for the first time, Wafa (already with her arm bandaged after a fall on the school stairs), her mother Amel, and her brother Shahdi, ventured out to see their home's remains.

Wafa was 70 metres from her home, and 800m from the border fence. Her mother and brother were 300m away from her. There were three shots. A neighbour who was 900m away says they were fired from two army jeeps and he saw a soldier shooting from the top of one. The first two bullets hit the ground beside Wafa. The third destroyed her kneecap, and she collapsed. Amel immediately thought she was dead. Shahdi tore off his white shirt to wave at the soldiers and began to move towards his sister.

'Don't go! She's dead! Come back!' his mother cried. The soldier began to direct further shots at Shahdi and his makeshift white flag and he couldn't continue, so he phoned for the ambulance. The ambulance was there within ten minutes, but before it got there, the jeeps had left and Shahdi was able to reach his sister and meet the ambulance with her in his arms.

Is there often shooting from the Israeli soldiers across the border into Khoza'a, we ask?

'*Kulyoom!*' everyone choruses – Every day. Various villagers tell us about life in Khoza'a.

'Along the border, there are normally two jeeps and a tank every 500m. And every 2½ km, there is a gate they can drive tanks through to our side if they want. And they have put microphones on the border

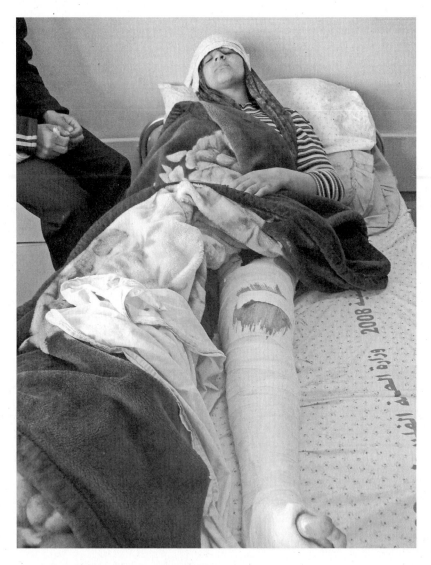

6.3 17 year old Wafa was shot in the knee on February 25 as she visited the remains of her Khoza'a house with her mother and brother.

Sharyn Lock

fence, so they can play the sound of barking dogs at us, and shout at us, as well as the shooting.'

'We often see women soldiers,' someone adds.

'In the December/January war, 25 were martyred (killed) and 70 injured. In the first days the army didn't let the ambulance reach us so people died from small injuries. But before that, in the past five years, we had 130 killed in Khoza'a by Israel – from shooting, from attacks.'

Various people start talking about the Khoza'a school. It was built in 2003, after the Oslo accords, exactly one mile from the border, as a result of an agreement between Yasser Arafat and Israeli Defence Minister Ehud Barak. Prior to that, the children had 8km to walk to get to a neighbouring school.

Since then, it's been bombed twice and occupied by Israeli soldiers at least once. This is a school that serves 380 girls, 400 boys, and 800 pre-schoolers, starting at 6.30am and finishing at 6.30pm, holding two school shifts. But currently, the shooting directed at it is so intense that the kids spend a lot of their time on the floor, and only a handful of lessons take place each day.

Why the shooting?

'The reason the Israeli army gives publicly is, because resistance fighters are firing from behind the school.'

And are they?

'No.' Everyone is very clear on that point.

'In the past, lots of people from Gaza would come to visit Khoza'a. It is the eastern-most point of Gaza. And the Najar family is one of two very big, very well respected families here.'

'It took us eight years to build our house. We only lived in it for nine months. And we so wanted to see what was left of it. I just had to see it,' says Amel. 'Other people had walked into that area since the war, but we hadn't, not until yesterday.'

Why did she and Shahdi and Wafa go yesterday in particular?

'We heard there were internationals in the area.'

Oh no. Eva, Ewa, and I look at each other, hearts sinking. We clarify.

They didn't have any particular information – it was just a rumour – there were internationals around, maybe that meant a delegation of important people, maybe that meant something was arranged with Israel via the Red Cross, maybe that meant it was safer than a normal day, maybe things for once would be ok.

But they weren't. Because the internationals were us. Getting shot at with the farmers. Just like a normal Khoza'a day. Only for Wafa, so much worse.

A couple of people want to tell us something else. Something they want in Khoza'a. Ewa translates again. They have a lot of doctors and other health care workers living there, they say. Maybe as many as 30. Beside Wafa's bed now are two of them, a young male nurse and another young man who volunteers here at Nasser. And everyone is hoping that maybe, one day soon, some funding organisation from the outside world would help them build a Khoza'a hospital.

They have it exactly right. They have a much better chance that some country, some international organisation somewhere, will give them money for a hospital to treat their wounded closer to home, than that any country, any international organisation, will stand up to Israel and stop Khoza'a's children being wounded in the first place.

MARCH 3

Last night Eva and I went to visit Amer and Shireen Al Helou, and surviving kids Saja, Foad, and Mahmoud.[4] They are back in their Zaytoun house,[5] which looks like a home again inside, instead of the disaster area the Israeli soldiers occupying it left behind. Shireen showed us the cupboards full of scrubbed folded clothes, all of which had been left soiled. It was a relief to Eva and me to see everyone there, in their proper place with their belongings around them. Amer's now-widowed mother is living with them, and his younger sisters too.

But all the mirrors that are carefully back on the wall are cracked, and the ceiling still has holes in, and the clean folded clothes in the smallest cupboard belong to Farah, who will never wear them again. And at the top of the stairs is a new, framed martyr poster, showing the faces of baby Farah, her grandfather, and her uncle Mohammed (who died elsewhere, one of several hundred resistance fighters killed during the invasion, compared to around 1,000 civilians). And her other uncle Abdullah is in the next room, subdued under many blankets, slowly recovering from the multiple gunshot wounds he sustained in the attack that killed Farah and her grandfather and wounded Saja.

Not that they have a choice, but I cannot comprehend how this family can go about their daily lives feeling at home in a place where such horrible things happened to them. Run outside and play, kids. Where you all hid in terror under the stairs as they shelled your house, and then watched the soldiers shoot your grandfather and leave him to bleed to death.

In the photo albums we look at, after the photos of Foad's birthday when everyone was still alive and all was well, there is a photo of the reduced family of five from only weeks ago, looking stunned and disoriented. But the kids have remembered how to smile and laugh since I saw them last. And in a land where all the children are traumatised, they are normal. While the boys climb all over their dad, Saja is practising her handwriting, extraordinarily neat for her age, to strengthen her right arm again as it heals from the bullet. It appears that all will be well and she won't need further surgery.

Amer and Shireen showed us their wedding album (every Palestinian family's most treasured possession) and told us about how they were married. Shireen was 16, Amer 20. It was an arranged marriage. They both figured if their parents said the other was the right one for them, then all would be well. 'My mum said, you'll love her, and I said, good, *khalas*!' says Amer. (*Khalas* means literally 'enough' or 'stop', but I guess I'd translate it here as 'that's sorted then'.) They were engaged within a week, and married a month or so later. In their wedding photos

they are both devastatingly good looking, and you can see they are
both thinking – how lucky am I!

But more to the point, they are so clearly right for each other, so
clearly proud of and deeply attached to each other, so quietly glad to
be round each other, I am surprised once again to hear it wasn't a love
match. I'll have to get over this because it keeps happening. Head nurse
Khalid and his wife Sahar had an arranged marriage too. They have the
same dynamic. I guess if you marry young, straight from home, your
parents may very well know who you are and who you will do well
with. And then you and your partner do your growing and changing
with time, together.

I dropped in to visit Khalid at Al Quds hospital the other night on
the way to my ambulance shift. He said he is not sure why his family
hasn't received any government or UNRWA payout (modest though
it would be) towards their damaged house, so uninhabitable that they
are still living with his father.

He has managed to do some repairs on the house in the free time
his three jobs allow him. However, it is raining as we speak, and he
comments wryly that the rain will be falling *inside* the house. He
follows this with the characteristic bemused yet cheerful laugh that I
remember well from the Al Quds ICU (as if he feels that all you can
do with this whole insane situation is laugh at it) and a thank-you to
Allah that the family are all alive and uninjured. I met his two beautiful
little daughters Jasmeen and Sawsun, and his lovely wife, shortly after
the so-called ceasefire when I visited them for lunch.

Today as I left the First Responder medic course in Khan Younis,
the ground rocked with an explosion, more felt than heard. Fida
helpfully texted me minutes later with 'Israeli warplanes bombed
tunnel in As-Salam neighbourhood of Rafah, no casualties reported.'
However we heard originally that there were no injuries from
yesterday's seven airstrikes in the same area, but now Al Jazeera says
four people were injured. Ma'an News, which can be entirely accurate
or entirely inaccurate, says 'Palestinian medical sources at Abu Yousif

An-Najjar Hospital in Rafah said 12 Palestinians were injured in Tuesday's shelling.'

We also heard that in recent days there were six injuries and one death down the tunnels from Egyptian forces spraying teargas down them, something they do regularly. I've not been able to confirm this. We heard that the young man who died was 22, putting himself through college and supporting his parents with his tunnel digging wage.

Aside from the weapons smuggling through the tunnels that Israel uses to justify these attacks (I guess the US only does weapons home-delivery for Israel, and Hamas find it hard to get to London for the DSEI arms fair) these tunnels bring us food and baby milk and clothes and many of the other things which Israel hasn't let into Gaza in any amount for years. Most of us eat because of these tunnels, those of us who can afford to buy food. The rest eat because of the few UNRWA aid trucks Israel lets through. But they don't eat very much, because of all the UNRWA aid trucks Israel *doesn't* let through. Thousands of trucks have been sitting at the border.

I was down on the shore again tonight for sunset. Here are the fishermen out as usual, to catch fish or bullets, as fate and Israel would have it.

Faraheen farmers were fired on again yesterday; we weren't with them.

By the way, after all the sleepless nights of shelling, the Kabariti girls finished their first semester exams with impressively high marks: 94.4 for Sara, 98.6 for Suzanne, and 99 for Fatma!

MARCH 6

Yesterday, along with my friend Rama, I went along to the second day of the new kids' play space, set up in the temporary (*insha'allah*) Samoud Camp in the ruins of Jabalia's Hay Salaam area. Ewa and Caoimhe have partnered up with local youth leaders to put the space together, naming it after the Free Gaza project, and using one-off donations from various folks outside to buy (scarce and hard to obtain) tents, toys and snacks for the kids.

Children from about 5 to 12 crowded excitedly in the dust outside the gate, then headed into the separate girls and boys tents, only stopping to fling off their shoes at the doorways. Most of them come from houses now flattened or no longer even locatable, and their families are attempting to live in temporary shelters or tent towns such as Samoud, which are too small for the number of homeless and have few facilities. The tents didn't look up to the job when I first saw them, and are looking even more forlorn now after recent rain, snow, and strong winds.

After some games, the youth leaders asked some to come singly into the circle centre and tell their stories from the attacks and what had happened to their families. Rama translated.

'When they said that the troops will enter our area by tanks, no one could sleep. It was the longest night we ever had. There was no electricity, no lights, there was nothing but the sound of the rockets and bombing around us. Dad said that we should read Quran and pray and that's what we did all the night! I couldn't close my eyes and couldn't stand up. It was a very frightening night. In the morning, Dad said, we're going to leave our house and go to our uncle's house because it is safer. Dad and my brother carried white flags and we followed them. Even though, the tanks did not stop firing on us and we started running.'

'We also left our house carrying the white flags and they were shooting but we ran faster than the ambulances!'

Rama wrote later:

The play space was like heaven in the middle of the fire… it is very simple but it was another world… I felt I wanted to cry and hug those little bodies. If you heard them, you'd wish to carry them between your arms. However, when they tell the stories, you feel that they are very strong and this is a normal thing. They laugh, play, speak loudly and strongly. This play space is giving them the opportunity to have a normal kids' life even for 2 hours…

MARCH 12

With me in the taxi back from Al Fukhari tonight, Eva is on the phone checking if we can visit Abd[6] tomorrow in Al Wafa hospital to deliver a chess set. '*Fil asr*,' she finishes.

'Isn't "*asr*" Arabic for afternoon?' I ask.

'Well, maybe. Unless it's the word for honey,' she says thoughtfully.

'No, that's *asal*,' I say.

'And as long as it's not the word for juice.'

'No, that's *asir*.'

'Then if I didn't say we'd meet him in the honey or in the juice, I probably said we'd meet him in the afternoon.'

We were visiting hospital dietician Saleh's family in Al Fukhari. They fled their home during the attacks, except for Saleh's dad who stayed behind to confront the tanks. Which he literally did – Saleh shows us where the tanks got to: the back garden. At this point, his dad went to the back door and looked the soldier in the tank in the eye. The soldier in the tank looked back. And then he turned the tank around and left. I guess Abu Saleh has one hell of a stern look.

As we are leaving we pass several houses totally destroyed, in amongst houses still standing. Why these houses? Nobody knows. A kindergarten is also destroyed, and there is no logic in that either. We notice that all the roads are planted with dense cacti, and speculate if they are deliberately planted to obstruct border-originating bullets. They look fierce enough to do it. At Saleh's family land, near the border, Israeli tanks have destroyed the roadside cacti, so maybe the soldiers have the same theory about them as us.

Earlier in the afternoon we were with Sobhe and Yara and their six kids (the youngest is 3) in Al Faraheen. They stay in a house in the middle of the village now, because their regular home at the edge, about 500m from the border, feels too dangerous. Before the attacks, Sobhe and his oldest son at least were sleeping at their farmhouse. Now, no-one does.

6.4   The children of Yara and Sobhe. Yara was injured while working at the Faraheen farmhouse they'd left as too dangerous.
Sharyn Lock

Before the war when ISMers were visiting, the Israeli army seemed to be trying to enforce (by shooting) a 300m no-go zone on the Palestinian side of the border. At the time, Sobhe said he was afraid it would shortly turn into a 500m no-go zone. After the December/January attacks, when Eva rang the Canadian embassy to tell them she was with Palestinians being fired on while picking parsley, the Canadian officials said something along the lines of 'Israel says you are in the 1km no-go zone.' The *what*? And who made them the boss of the world? – as we used to say as kids. And does this remind anyone of how the government in Orwell's *1984* rewrites 'facts' regularly and then everyone colludes to say those were *always* the facts?

What I didn't realise until today is that Sobhe and Yara are paying $100 a month rent for the village house, out of their small farming income. In the hope some compensation money might be available from UNRWA, Sobhe asks us to take photos of the damage to their house and help them contact the appropriate authorities.

A few minutes later, at the farmhouse, Sobhe points out the 'donkey radar' – a donkey in the field on the border side, nose pointing towards Israel – insisting that the donkey's ears will go up if jeeps arrive. It is easy to tell Sobhe's heart and soul are in farming and he loves his land. He practises crop rotation on the remaining 4 dunums, close to the house, that it seems worth risking his life to access. In the past he shared 300 dunums (a dunum is about 1,000 square metres) with his brothers and neighbours – 3 dunums were olives, 6 were fruit trees, 50 were wheat, 50 were peas... Israel totally destroyed the fruit trees in previous incursions and since the rest of the land goes all the way up to the border, he has given up on it.

Before the army incursion in May 2008, he also had 3,000 chickens, but the army killed 2,500 of them, also destroying 30 pieces (each 1m x 2.5m) of shed roofing, breaking his tractor and his wheat picker (worth about US$12,000), breaking the pump for his well, and shooting up his kitchen fridge, water tank, solar water heater, self-designed solar dryer, and the walls of the house.

The remaining 500 chickens died in January 2009 after eating plants poisoned by phosphorus bombs, and another 30 pieces of shed roofing went the way of the first lot. Sobhe had to destroy a crop of radishes still in the field when he realised they'd been similarly poisoned. What this will do long term to his land, no-one knows. The family's TV and computer were also destroyed in the December attacks when shelling caused part of the roof to fall in on top of them.

Now I am writing from a few hours on ambulance shift. There is a new ambulance, a present from Germany. I notice its siren can be set to 'wail' or 'yelp' (this reminds me of my friend's washing machine, that can be set to 'very dirty', 'medium dirty' or 'little dirty', which makes so much more sense to me than the 'light coloureds non fast' nonsense on machines in the UK). I also notice that, like all ambulance radios here, the radio seems only to play the theme song from *Titanic*, a big Arabic favourite.

I was here Tuesday, and it was quiet, so I practised inserting a cannula in the arm of ten years' ambulance veteran Adel, making the classic yet entertaining mistake of removing the cannula needle *before* taking the tourniquet off instead of *after* – this results in blood spurting everywhere. I didn't feel too bad as the last person I saw make that mistake was someone with a year's nursing training behind her. Upon asking where the medical waste disposal was, I was told – out the window. During the war, since no medical waste collection was possible, it simply went out into the enclosed Red Crescent compound, and no collection service has yet been available.

People from the VivaPalestina convoy are in town, after an epic journey and having battled their way through Rafah, the day after the CodePink folks were able to do the same. Not being a sane rational person, but someone who isn't happy in crowds or around cameras, I've not actually gone to say hello. But tomorrow I will meet up with some to help introduce them to whatever medics are on ambulance shift so their stories can be heard. Caoimhe and Ewa, who have been doing great work pointing them towards good contacts here and helping with translation, have said the convoy has a large proportion of down-to-earth working class folks, Muslim and otherwise, which makes a good change from us burnt-out activist types.

And in Egypt, Fatah and Hamas are talking their way towards a Unity government again, we hope...

Ewa and Caoimhe are living with me for the moment. We still don't have gas, but Ewa has bought an electric ring, so we can finally make tea – which Andrew and Stelios keep giving us boxes of. 'Why all this tea?' I ask. 'It comes free with the loo roll,' says Stelios. He shows me a packet of toilet roll – with, sure enough, a box of tea attached. 'And I guess we drink less tea than we... well, anyway, we have more than we need.'

Having Ewa and Caoimhe around keeps my spirits up. After years of Palestinian and Iraqi living the culture has sunk in, and they always arrive everywhere, including home, with fruit or traditional sweets which they insist on everyone in the vicinity eating. With fluent Arabic, they are taking on far more horrific stories daily than I am, and giving back compassion and strength. Ewa tells me, 'The word *intifada*, resistance, it doesn't just mean direct action, it means surviving, keeping hope alive, holding onto joy. It's the work you do in your own heart too.'

Eva, however, is my partner for daily work, just enough ahead of me in language to stretch me, always ready with a smile. Sometimes she feels like my other self – the same recognition I felt when Vik and I first met – even to a love of Australian cartoonist Michael Leunig. Every day we are together; visiting, documenting, and then meeting each other's eye when exhaustion starts to overwhelm the ability to listen and comprehend, when we have to escape. Then we relocate to the internet cafe where we sit for hours opposite each other in companionable silence, intent on our laptops, attempting to write stories that do justice to pain and courage. Eva doesn't just give money to an old man begging; she starts a conversation, follows him home, learns his story, writes about him, finds what assistance can be found. No-one is a statistic to Eva. She is loved here.

MARCH 13

I have just been in touch with West Bank ISMer Adam to find out how ISMer Tristan is doing, after he was severely injured yesterday when the tear gas canister an Israeli soldier shot at his head punctured his skull. Apparently he is still in a critical condition and has had to have the front part of his brain removed. If he makes it through the next 48 hours his chances of survival increase. There will be long-term effects but not clear yet how severe.

Tristan is an activist and Indymedia journalist. The local man shot in the leg with live ammunition at the same time as Tristan was hit is ok and back at home in Ni'lin now.

When we think about the danger we sometimes face (always less than Palestinians) we hope for the clean, quick bullet. And try not to think about the alternatives. I don't know Tristan myself. He seems like a nice guy in the photo, which looks to be the photo we all hand in for use 'in case something happens'.

There have been attacks from sky and sea all week, mostly focused on the tunnels which feed us, but not all. Yesterday I went to the Kabariti family for Friday lunch, a fish barbeque. I took with me three of the 'letters from the world' that were delivered by the Free Gaza boat last year. These letters were from a mother and her two daughters in California, so we decided to give them to the Kabariti girls and their mum, all of whom read English.

The girls and I sat in the sunny front window and they excitedly began to read their letters and compose messages to email in reply (no postal service is possible under siege). A few minutes later I realised I could hear shooting. Their dad Mahfouz always keeps binoculars beside the sea window, but I didn't need them. Looking out, I could see two Israeli gunboats well on this side of the horizon, looping about and firing on Palestinian fishing boats. No more than three miles from the shore.

Some of the little boats began to head back to port, so I stomped off down the street to meet them, as the shooting continued, to see what I could find out. I spoke to Ahmed Abel Aziiz, who had just tied up his boat. He said the shooting had been going on half an hour and he was giving up for the day, but he thought that more than ten boats, some medium and some small like his, were still out there. Nobody was arrested or wounded yet. I stomped back to eat my lunch, pleased to see the Kabariti kids out in the garden after their weeks of hiding inside, but eyeing the parsley in the salad and the fish on my plate with part respect and part despair.

Later on I rang Mahfouz and he said that fishermen Zaki Tarouch, Talal Tarouch and Dahr Zayad and his son, had been arrested by the Israeli gunboats. He also said we are entering the three best months for fishing, the time the fishermen depend on to get them through the rest of the year.

We went to Al Wafa rehabilitation hospital also yesterday, said hi to Abd, delivered the chess set our blog donations bought him, and announced we would be practising both chess and insertion of cannulas on him next visit. He looked perturbed. Eva introduced me to Abd's fellow patient, Maher, who is carrying on the Palestinian tradition of being determinedly cheerful after surviving his own war nightmare. Which in his case involved not only losing those close to him, but ten minutes in the morgue refrigerator after being pronounced dead...

The fishermen were released in the night, but their boats – their method of earning a living – have been impounded by Israel. As we enter the three months Gaza fishermen depend on the most.

MARCH 16

Our two Rafah ISM colleagues (both of whom worked with Rachel) invited us south for a commemoration kite-flying today; one kite to commemorate Rachel Corrie who was killed by Israel on this day in

2003,[7] and 14 kites to commemorate over 1,400 Palestinians killed by Israel in December 2008/January 2009. They also invited local artists to paint a section of the Israeli wall near where Rachel was killed.

The kids flying the kites had a great time, but for us it felt sadly ironic to be doing this while awaiting news of Tristan. In our medic class this morning we were practising responding to a head injury, and very clear in our thoughts were the images of Tristan's broken head just after his shooting.

Anarchists Against the Wall, a mainly Israeli group which supports Palestinian resistance against the Separation Wall on West Bank land, provided more details on the 13th:

> Tristan is unconscious, anaesthetized and artificially respirated, has sustained life-threatening injuries to his brain, and is expected to undergo several operations in the coming days, in addition to the one today.
>
> The impact of the projectile caused numerous condensed fractures to Anderson's forehead and right eye socket. During the operation, part of his right frontal lobe had to be removed, as it was penetrated by bone fragments. A brain fluid leakage was sealed using a tendon from his thigh, and both his right eye and skin suffered extensive damage. The long-term scope of all of Tristan's injuries is yet unknown.
>
> It should also be noted that soldiers at the Ni'ilin checkpoint prevented the Red Crescent ambulance from taking Tristan directly to the hospital, forcing it to wait for approximately 15 minutes until an Israeli ICU ambulance (called by Israeli activists) arrived at the scene, after which he had to be carried from one ambulance to the other. This, of course, is standard procedure – in the extremely rare cases where the army allows patients from the occupied territories to be transferred into Israel.

In the taxi on our way home from Rafah, the man in the seat in front, from Beit Lahia, showed us photos of his three children on his phone. He said something about 'phosphorus'. 'They were all burnt with the phosphorus bombs?' I asked, looking at those little faces.

He shook his head, I hadn't understood. They were all killed.

A couple of days ago, I made contact with Maher, a clinical psychologist from the Palestine Trauma Centre. The 14 year old in the family of our Jabalia friends whose mother Sara was killed in the first ten minutes of the December 27 attacks is frightened to ever be alone, even for a moment, and I wanted to see what support is available. I am also worried about another family member, Fatima's small nephew Abdullah, who bursts into tears whenever he hears tank fire – as he did the last time we visited a few weeks ago. He has been traumatised to some extent ever since his father's legs were blown off several years ago, and the recent hiding in the basement under bombing then fleeing their home hasn't helped.

The PTC has only been fairly recently formed, and during the attacks its university trained therapists were in the field, 32 of them, based for example in the UNRWA schools-turned-refuges. Maher told me about one woman they did their best to help. Her family were in their house in 'Atatra when it was shelled. Her husband was decapitated by an explosion in front of her. Her four children were set on fire by phosphorus bombs and died begging her for help she couldn't give, but she sustained third-degree burns trying.

When the PTC people first met her shortly afterwards she was not sleeping, but awake 24 hours a day, weeping and calling for someone to help her children – who in her head were still alive and burning. After two weeks working with her, they took her to the graves of the children, to show her they were really gone. The therapists knew that, due to her burns and the possibility of contamination, they should do their best to prevent her from touching the earth of the graves. But of course she fell to the ground and tried to find some way to gather her children into her arms.

Another patient they have been working with, a 13 year old, didn't lose her family, but her room and all her belongings were burnt. When she saw what was left, she quietly began to eat the ashes.

Later, I was listening to some Palestinians talking about the attacks. 'What do you think we learnt from this time?' one asked.

'It should teach us to stick together more,' the other answered.

I so wouldn't be asking myself that question, or giving myself that answer, if I'd just gone through what these people have. For sure, there are some Gaza people I've met who I don't like. I also know that because I only understand a little bit of Arabic, my experience of some people's personalities is smoothed over, and so maybe I get on with people easier than I might if I knew more of the details. But. There is still so very much that moves me about this community.

We now have a security liaison person, Abu Qusai, who was one of the few survivors pulled from the rubble of his police station on December 27. (Our first security liaison person, Hamse, is dead.) In his first meeting with us after the attacks, he went through the business stuff first, quietly, looking like you would if most of your colleagues had recently been crushed to death around you. After thanking us, and telling us the meeting was finished, he paused a moment and said, with what I can only describe as a kind of polite, almost humble bewilderment, 'Can I ask a question, just a personal one, outside the meeting? What you saw...in these weeks...do people outside know what happens to Palestinians? Is this on the television outside?'

And we thought of all those bodies. And the kids shot at point blank. And we thought of bomb after bomb after bomb falling, every day for weeks. And we thought of the sanitised minutes that in our experience are given to Palestine footage.

'No. The media doesn't show what we saw.'

And he nodded, thoughtfully, then squared his shoulders, ready to set off. I could see we'd only confirmed his own belief. Many people here quietly, yet sturdily, carry this belief that – to the outside world – they don't really matter. But they just don't understand why.

My friend Joe writes from America...

Today is the 6 year anniversary of the murder of my friend and comrade Rachel Corrie. I was with her when she was crushed to death by a US-made Caterpillar Israeli Military Bulldozer as she stood nonviolently protecting a Palestinian civilian home. There are memorial services happening all over the country.

He's written a poem for Rachel today; here are some words from it:

...So many remember you, but forget the thousands of Palestinians
They remember you but have never heard of Tom, or James, or
Nabila or Ali...
As I've traveled this land speaking of your last stand
Still clutching to your hand, extending out of the sand
I accept that I cannot pull you out
But we
Might keep the rest of us
From being pulled under...[8]

MARCH 19

We were back at Faraheen this morning accompanying farmers again, eyeing the jeeps driving along the border while our farmers removed the irrigation pipes from one of the fields we have visited regularly. Since Mohammed was shot in the leg, the farmer here has decided to give up on this field, its convenient well, and its half-grown parsley crop – 200,000 shekels worth – in case of further injury or death. It was a quiet morning, thank goodness.

Tristan is conscious and was breathing on his own until he caught pneumonia. He has a long way to go and it's not known what will be ahead – for sure, more surgery, including on his damaged right eye.

I met a great Manchester guy this week, Dr Sohail of MIST (Mobile International Surgical Team) who has come here to work with peoples' bones, for example working with amputees who have had limbs removed high up, to enable the otherwise impossible attachment of prosthetic limbs (if Israel lets the prosthetics through the border, another problem of the siege).

Thinking about bones, I immediately thought of Wafa. After wincing at the picture of her in hospital the day after soldiers shot out her kneecap, Dr Sohail said: 'I'm a kneecap man!' and told me a series of incomprehensible surgical things he might be able to do to give her back some movement. We rang her family today while standing in the Faraheen field (it's a good time to get your phone-calling done) to say that Dr Sohail will see her in June if I take a photo of her medical records for him beforehand.

Dr Sohail spoke of the several limitations medical people are under here: mostly no access to the latest equipment – if any gets in, no access to training on how to use it – and of course very little of the ongoing training amongst their international peers that surgeons need to have.

In the last days there have been renewed calls for an International Criminal Court investigation into war crimes in Gaza, including 'white flag killings' by Israeli soldiers. One of the big problems is that during the attacks, there were no forensic pathologists in Gaza trained to a sufficient level (they are trying to send some people outside for training now, ready for the next time...). A second big problem is that when the International Criminal Court representatives tried to get in through Rafah to investigate, Egypt refused to let them through, so they missed the February 8 deadline for submitting evidence.

And it was never going to be easy. Here is an example. One of the Al Quds Red Crescent medics talked about reaching some of the surviving Samouni kids trapped with dead adults, on the first Red Cross/Red Crescent evacuation permitted by Israel. He said the kids (who they found in circumstances that left some of the medics traumatised

White flag killings

In August 2009, Human Rights Watch reported allegations of 'white flag killings' by Israeli forces. The human rights NGO's final publication detailed 'seven incidents where Israeli soldiers fired on civilians with small arms during Israel's major military operations in Gaza in December 2008 and January 2009. These attacks killed eleven civilians – including five women and four children – and wounded at least another eight.'

'These casualties comprise a small fraction of the Palestinian civilians killed and wounded during what Israel called Operation Cast Lead,' Human Rights Watch continued, 'but they stand out because of the circumstances of the attacks. In each case, the victims were standing, walking, or in a slowly moving vehicle with other unarmed civilians who were trying to convey their noncombatant status by waving a white flag. All available evidence indicates that Israeli forces had control of the areas in question, no fighting was taking place there at the time, and Palestinian fighters were not hiding among the civilians who were shot.'

Human Rights Watch interviewed multiple witnesses to each event, visited the attack sites, examined ballistic evidence and collected medical records. It also directed repeated questions to the IDF, which declined to answer them.

The cases documented by Human Rights Watch include that of Khalid Abed Rabbu, described on page 129, whose two young daughters were killed and their grandmother and a third daughter wounded while they were carrying white flags. Other cases include Nada al-Marrdi, age 5, Mattar Sa'ad Abu Halima, 17, Muhammad Hikmat Abu Halima, 16 and Ibrahim Mu'in Juha, 14. Human Rights Watch also criticised comments such as those of IDF Colonel Liron Liebman, who called demands for investigations into the actions of Israeli soldiers in Gaza 'legal terrorism'.

Reference: Human Rights Watch, 'White flag deaths: killings of Palestinian civilians during Operation Cast Lead', August 2009.

themselves) said the adults had been shot, and they had covered over the bodies themselves.

The medics knew it was important to try to take the adults' bodies out, but the children were starving, dehydrated, and in a state of collapse. Since Israel had not permitted the medics to take ambulances, and several miles had to be covered, the medics found a donkey cart for the children. The Red Cross asked Israel to be allowed to take a donkey to pull the cart, but Israel said no.

My medic friend says: 'We put the children on the donkey cart and pulled it ourselves, hurrying to get out before 4pm which was the deadline for the evacuation. And there was no room for the bodies. So a lot of time passed before those bodies could be retrieved, and while we have the verbal testimony of the children, we don't have an early medical assessment of the adults' bodies.'

7
MARCH 23–APRIL 20, 2009
'Badri!'

MARCH 23

'Fire also upon rescue'.

This is what it said in the 'how to run an Israeli incursion' notes an IOF commander appears to have left behind (doh) near Jabalia.[1] Just in case the Gaza medics thought being shot at was accidental. I shouldn't read the online comments that follow articles like this that try to speak out within Israel, but inevitably I do... and it's funny how half of them appear to be from such ignorant and racist Zionists that all by themselves they totally provide the answer to the 'how could anyone possibly believe Israelis would do this' comments posted by others. And the commenters who ask that question – what bubble do they live in? Do they not watch the news? Do they not read my blog, for goodness sake?!

Some of the good guys – Israeli Physicians for Human Rights – released a report today stating that 'Israel attacked 34 medical care facilities and prevented Palestinian medical teams from reaching the wounded during the offensive in December and January.'

Some more of the good guys, Anarchists Against the Wall, who've no doubt been keeping Tristan and his family as cushioned as they can in his Israeli hospital room, gave us a new update yesterday and it isn't good.

March 22 update: There has been some deterioration in Tristan's condition over the weekend, and he has had to undergo two more emergency brain surgeries due to elevated cerebral pressure. Tristan's condition is now once more defined critical and unstable, and he is fighting for his life. Tristan's parents and lawyer will hold a press conference in Jerusalem tomorrow afternoon.

The press conference was reported by the Alternative Information Centre, and seeing Tristan's parents' faces has filled my eyes with tears, here in this Gaza net cafe where I have the least right to cry of anyone.

And Ma'an News (which is sometimes wrong but has a good chance of being right this time) says another fisherman was shot from Israeli gunboats a couple of hours ago, 18 year old Muhammad Al-Lawwah, somewhere near the beach I go walking on. And Deeb Al Ankaa, who was injured last Tuesday March 17, who my colleagues visited yesterday, tells us he was just *10 metres* from the beach when he was shot twice, once in the shoulder and once in the torso where the bullet has left both entry and exit wounds. He's been married eight months. And his father was 40m from the shore when he had his little boat confiscated on the same day.

I don't really know what to say today. I can't make all this injury and death into something hopeful, or something meaningful, or even something *interesting*. It's grindingly everyday.

I will leave you with something I discovered a little while ago. Remember before the ground incursion began, when Eva and I were spending nights with our Jabalia friends as they hid in the basement while the bombs fell? And how we would go out in the morning (somewhat fewer bombs) to document the attacks? And how we took a picture of a yellow truck in which a family had been blown up?[2]

Well, what I didn't know was that Israel was actually using footage of the last minutes of these people's lives, taken from the air, as a propaganda video about how they were just targeting Hamas rocket firers. However, the locals told a B'Tselem field worker the same story they told us and a very different version of events was posted to YouTube.

The 'yellow truck' incident

In the first days of the attack on Gaza, the Israeli military released footage of a truck, laden with alleged Hamas rockets, being destroyed by a 'precision' missile strike from a Predator drone.

Within days, however, Israeli human rights NGO B'Tselem announced that it had interviewed witnesses to the incident, who said instead that the truck was a civilian vehicle moving gas welding canisters from a metalworking shop.

The *Guardian* newspaper reported that 'The pictures released by B'Tselem yesterday – which it says were taken at the site – show the burnt-out wreckage of a truck that appears to have been loaded with scrap metal and gas welding tanks, with the gas valves still attached. An undamaged tank, apparently thrown out of the vehicle by the explosion, is identical in shape to the burned ones.'

The truck's owner, Ahmad Sanur, insisted that he had never been involved with Hamas militants, and gave the names of those killed in the strike as Muhammad Bassel Madi, 17, Wisam Akram Eid, 14, Imad Ahmad Sanur, 32, Rami Sa'adi Ghabayan, 24, Mahmoud Nabil Ghabayan, 14, Ashraf al-Dabagh, 26, Muhammad Majed Ka'abar, 20, and Ahmad Ibrahim Khila, 15. Imad was Ahmad Sanur's son.

References: *Guardian*, '"Eight civilians killed" in surgical strike on truck', January 1, 2009; Human Rights Watch, 'Precisely wrong: Gaza civilians killed by Israeli drone-launched missiles', June 2009.

Thinking about Jabalia has reminded me of something hopeful, after all. Our Jabalia friends have told us the family will be expecting a new baby later this year. If it's a girl, she will be called after her grandmother Sara, who died while out seeking bread for her grandchildren, on December 27 when the sky fell in on Gaza. For a country that loves its children so much, and yet loses so many, this is the one kind of hope you can pick up and hold tight.[3]

I wonder if we will get to keep Tristan, too?

I wonder if Tristan, who doctors say may have to contend with severe disabilities, wants to stay?

MARCH 31

Today we accompanied farmers in the Latamat area on the outskirts of Khoza'a. The last time we were out farming in Khoza'a the shooting was the closest I'd experienced, and from the video footage it looked like the Israelis were aiming to shoot Jenny in the leg.

Since later that same day Wafa was shot in the kneecap, and not too long before that farmer Mohammed was shot in the foot while we were with him, the ISM group had been taking stock. We decided that Gaza ISM had to hold meetings with any farmers that wanted our accompaniment and be absolutely sure they understood that our presence protects them only mildly, if at all.

My personal feeling was that as long as they are clear on that, then if they still want us we should go, but then I have to leave Gaza soon. In the Khoza'a meeting (this included showing our video footage of the Faraheen shooting of Mohammed and telling them about Tristan's shooting and the past killings of ISMers) the farmers replied 'Ok, maybe they shoot at us when you are with us, we're used to that because they shoot at us when you are not with us. So it's normal. But if you are with us when it happens – at least you can tell the world about it.'

So we met the mostly women farmers at 7am (often women work the most dangerous areas in the hope the soldiers will shoot less) and walked to the fields which were about 400–500m from the border. Today's crop was lentils. I have never seen a lentil plant before, and I certainly hope no-one has to shell the lentils individually cos that would really be some job.

The farmers told us they had been shot at the day before in this same field. Several of us had had bad dreams the night before, and I'd written a quick will with various keepsakes for Gaza friends. In the van, Eva and I exchanged computer passwords and emergency contact numbers (actually, I've noticed her looking speculatively at me sometimes, since I told her she gets my laptop if something happens to me here). She also informed me that for her 'martyr poster' if she died, she wanted a picture of her with a donkey. So it was with some sense of doom that we walked down the track among golden wheatfields. And when explosions started shaking the ground, we wondered if we should even keep going. We rang Sobhe in Faraheen, since they seemed to be coming from his direction.

But he told us that actually what we could hear was a fight between Palestinian resistance and Israeli occupation forces in Magazi camp (where head nurse Khalid and his family live) which was a lot further north. So the lentil picking got underway and we tried to feel reassured by the fact that the F16s and Apaches flying overhead, and the distant roaring, were not directed at us. But I couldn't help imagining what it must be like to be a resistance fighter on the ground facing that formidable firepower.

Anyway, it wasn't long before two jeeps turned up at the border, and Israeli soldiers got out. We waited for the inevitable, and it came – a short burst of shooting, only broadly in our direction. The women working on the ground tensed up and waited. But that turned out to be it. The soldiers got back in the jeeps and drove off again. Some hours later, lots of lentils were picked, the sun was high, everyone was relaxed, and the morning was a success. I discovered later that Stelios has cheekily finished the YouTube footage of the shooting with a minute or two of me and Eva entertaining ourselves with some of the *dubke* dance steps we've learnt.

Later we heard that in Magazi camp, two fighters were killed, two injured, and an Israeli soldier was injured and an Israeli jeep destroyed. I texted Khalid and asked how the little girls were. 'My children are used to bombing now,' he replied resignedly. I can't help but feel like the resistance fighters took the fire for us today. If Israel hadn't been busy shooting at them, from past experience it seems a sure thing they would have stuck round to shoot at us, like they had at the same farmers in the same place the day before. I guess that's why the resistance is called the resistance.

Later that afternoon, Vik and I were sitting smoking *shisha*, looking out at the sea, and gunfire got our attention again. Squinting, we spotted another Israeli gunship, tormenting another Palestinian fishing boat. The gunboat alternated tightly circling the fishing boat with drive-by shooting; we could see the spray as the bullets hit the water. It reminded me of nothing more than a cat playing with a mouse. This was still going on several hours later when we left.

Today, Eva heard that yesterday a woman she visited in Al Shifa hospital, Ghada, the 21 year old mum of two little girls, finally died in an Egyptian hospital of her horrendous white phosphorus burns; the phosphorus stripping her naked in the street before it ate her skin. Before she was sent out to Egypt she gave her testimony to Mohammed at the Red Crescent, who passed it to Israeli human rights organisation B'Tselem.

Oh…and Israel dropped its internal investigation into possible war crimes by the Israeli army in the December/January attacks.

APRIL 4

'Gazans to get soap next week, Israel announces,' Ma'an News informs us. And they've lifted the ban on those other dangerous substances, dates and pasta. Um, thanks Israel. Goodness knows what clean, date-eating Palestinians are going to get up to as a result.

APRIL 7

Today is World Health Day, and the World Health Organisation declared the theme for the day to be 'Save Lives: Make Hospitals Safe for Emergencies' (not bombing them would be a good start).

I made it over to Al Quds Red Crescent for the World Health Day ceremonies, held in the damaged middle building of the hospital complex. The highlight of this was the announcement of the winner of Palestine's short film competition on the above theme. All the films obviously focused on the Israeli attacks on hospitals and emergency workers, and the winning film, by Emad Badwan, included reference to medic Arafa's killing on January 4 as well as footage of medic Hassan's shooting by an Israeli sniper that my colleague Alberto took, and some voiceover by Eva who was there at the time. Mohammed Alruzzi's film included the following statement, something I guess we all vaguely know about...

Article 18 of the Geneva Convention (1949) states that civilian hospitals may in no circumstances be the object of attack but shall at all times be respected and protected by the Parties to the conflict.

Reading that, watching these clips, a sort of speeded up version of 22 insane days in which I took a small part, with a powerful soundtrack added, brought home to me in a way that somehow hadn't hit yet, just how ******* APPALLING those events were. Israel's December and January attacks didn't surprise me. The flechette shells, the white phosphorus, the horrific violence of the soldiers towards civilians, this just all seemed the logical result of us allowing the occupation of Palestine to continue at all.

If the world's governments let Israel break international law regularly, what would stop Israel continuing to do anything it wants? What would teach the soldiers to look at Palestinians and see their fellow humans? They already fire live ammunition at civilians in both the West Bank and Gaza, as a normal thing. Doing it on a larger scale, why not? The craziness of having to twice evacuate a hospital, and nightly work alongside terrified medics who had carried the bodies of their colleagues and expected to be the next dead, it just all seemed sickeningly logical to us at the time.

Today, the films allowed me to take a step back, to look from outside. After the ceremony, I went downstairs to look at the photographic exhibition which was also part of the World Health Day events, and was startled to find that four photos from my collection, which I'd handed over to the Red Crescent, had been enlarged and mounted as part of the exhibition. I found myself one step back, looking this time at literally exactly what I'd seen with my own eyes, what I'd paused for a few grudged seconds in the middle of the chaos to record, but not to think about. And thinking about it.

How did we let it happen? How did we? Why didn't I march out of that hospital and over to the apartment across the street holding the Israeli snipers that shot Haneen and her father as they ran towards the 'shelter' of Al Quds hospital and go up those stairs and JUST TAKE THOSE ****** GUNS OUT OF THEIR HANDS.

APRIL 9

As part of the World Health Day events, three artists are displaying their work in the same burnt-out theatre building as the concert last week, art that is a response to the Israeli attacks on hospitals and medical workers.

These buildings continue to come up with surprises for me. I got to know the main hospital building, and the basement of the Social Centre which in fact includes the hospital's emergency and obstetrics department, very well during the attacks. A small pedestrian bridge between the first and second buildings saves you going down the front steps of the first and up the front steps of the second, and we would cross this to smoke *shisha* in the smashed-up ground floor of the Social Centre during the war (as we weren't supposed to smoke in the hospital).

As the Israeli army line came closer and closer, and more often than not the Red Cross failed to obtain what is colloquially called *tanziiq*, or 'co-ordination', with Israel to collect the wounded civilians beyond the line of tanks, one of the Disaster Team joked that soon we'd have to call Israel to beg for co-ordination to cross this little pedestrian bridge for our *shisha* smoking.

I met with a couple of young women friends today, and we talked a little about that time. Medical student Duha spent many of the war days answering the Red Crescent phones, trying to tell parents and children how to stop their injured family members bleeding to death, since Israel was more willing to co-ordinate bullets than medical relief.

She told me about getting trapped in the nearby apartment her family had evacuated to, hiding in the basement with many other families, staying awake through the worst night with her brother. 'As the building rocked, we found ourselves listening to James Blunt's *Carry You Home*, with the lyrics...*as strong as you were, tender you go...I'm watching you breathing for the last time*. I told him to turn it off, that was really not what I wanted to hear right then!'

Nurse Raja told me a story I hadn't heard, about her pregnant fellow hospital worker, who became so frightened when the hospital was being bombed that she decided the best thing to do was descend to the hospital emergency/obstetrics department at basement level and not leave it. However shortly after she got there, the Israeli army's bullets started coming through the basement window (some time after, I filmed a short clip of the phosphorus fire reaching that department too).

It was Raja to whom we gave Yasmine Al Batran, in a state of terror having seen her 9 year old sister Haneen and her father Faddel shot by snipers, as the Israeli army shelled peoples' homes and fired upon them as they fled. It was Raja who listened to Faddel saying – 'It is all my fault, I thought the hospital would be safer than our house, I tried to bring them here', as he resisted treatment for his thigh wound, begging them only to save Haneen...who died of her abdomen and face wounds within hours.

I didn't realise the top floor of the Social Centre had a gym in it, until last week when Eva and I began meeting our former champion *tai kwon do* teacher there for our class, now that it has been vacated by the temporary clinic run by Moroccan doctors that arrived to assist with the war injured. I arrived before Eva, and found myself texting her to 'climb the stairs and turn left at the peacock'. On the way up the stairs I had been surprised to pass a small Natural History Museum, as well as the little cinema in which we watched yesterday's short films, and the gallery which housed the photo display, finally being greeted by a stuffed peacock on the gym level. There seem to be all sorts of other things in that building, including the Red Crescent youth volunteers' office.

Just before reaching the gym, I found myself under the open sky, surrounded by the burnt walls and cracked floor which are all that remains of the children's play space, destroyed when the roof was bombed with phosphorus.

What I write about these days is so little. For every story I have given you, there are a thousand others. I just spoke to Caoimhe, and she mentioned a Beit Hanoun family – Abu Harbid lost both legs going out to reach his dying oldest son, as an Israeli drone fired rockets at people in the street, killing and injuring many. He was a taxi driver so obviously now has no job; but does have eleven children. The oldest, who is 17 and has near-genius level intelligence, must give up school as he now has the best chance to earn a wage to feed them all... And there are all the things I don't tell you. I don't identify which of the injured young men I've written about has no reproductive organs anymore. I don't tell you which father cries secretly because he cannot provide for his children.

APRIL 11

Last night I was playing chess in the *shisha* cafe across from Al Quds Red Crescent, where I am sure to find a familiar face and where they seem to have got over me often being the only girl amongst the *shebab* (the lads), when I got a text from the south. 'Our friends Sobhe and Yara were trying to fix the asbestos sheeting on their farmhouse roof in Faraheen today...' it began.

I knew immediately that this message wasn't going to end well, and it didn't. At midday, three Israeli jeeps stopped and soldiers opened fire on Sobhe and Yara up on the roof of their home, firing about ten bullets. They tried to escape quickly down the stairs; but Yara, who already has a bad right leg, fell, breaking her left foot. Now she has a heavy plaster cast all the way from her toes to her knee.

When Eva and I visited them this morning in the rented house in the village. Yara was looking immobilised but determinedly cheerful, and sent us off to check on Sobhe, working at the farmhouse (being a farmer, he has little choice) and having already been fired on again today. Assuming the Israeli soldiers cared enough about who they are shooting at to bother checking, they would be able to confirm that Sobhe worked for years in Israel as an engineer (in fact as an inventor if we understand correctly). A peace mural decorates his living room wall. He is no threat to them, unless by his mere existence as a nonviolent Palestinian who loves his land.

I asked Sobhe something I'd always meant to – about Yara's bad right leg. It is twisted in a way that gives her an extremely pronounced limp, and I'd guessed it had been that way since birth. I was wrong.

During the First Intifada (1987–1991), there had been a nonviolent demonstration in Yara's village, beside her school, and the schoolchildren took part. Yara was 15. When Israeli soldiers started shooting tear gas into the crowd, Yara apparently decided they clearly couldn't be trusted with weapons. She and her friend Asan walked up to the nearest soldier, confiscated his M16 and threw it to the ground. A second soldier immediately killed Asan and shot Yara in the leg. Considering how I finished what I wrote on April 8, this story really had me looking at Yara with new respect. I thought about it; at half my age, she actually did it – disarming by direct action.

Sobhe insisted on driving us back to the village house, with his two little daughters, in the rickety trailer of a tiny tractor, one of the few working pieces of machinery recent attacks have left him. Bumping around, I was convinced we were about to tumble out.

'I'm too old for this sort of thing,' I said to Eva.

'I only got in because he winked!' she replied.

'As the actress said to the bishop,' I muttered, clinging on.

We drank tea at the village house, fielded the usual plans to get us married off to the locals to keep us firmly in the country, and then left for our next appointment, determined also to find Yara some crutches because she can't stand on either leg alone. Initial enquiries suggest this is something else there is a shortage of, especially since the war. The only option might be to buy her a pair, if we can find any.

After visiting medic Hassan and family in Khan Younis for lunch, Eva went back north to hunt for crutches, and I went south to join my ISM colleagues to attend a commemorative football game in memory of Tom Hurndall, who was shot in the head while rescuing a Palestinian child, on this day in 2003. We were all a bit tired and unenthusiastic, which I didn't feel so bad about, because I figure Tom would have known just how we felt; he too would have spent many a long day trying to alleviate Gaza's problems.

'If I die, I don't want any commemorative anything,' I decided. 'You can just think nice thoughts about me. In fact, I *require* you to think nice thoughts about me. And you can eat some chocolate in my memory.'

Actually, the game, held in the dust a few hundred yards from where Tom was shot, was really enjoyable despite cold weather and a smattering of rain. In Tom's name, Gaza ISM had provided a football, and a team's worth of T-shirts, and the Rafah locals were a lot of fun to watch. I especially enjoyed the small children wandering in a wobbly manner into the fray, heading delightedly for their fathers, uncles, and brothers; they would be swept up and deposited to the side, only to repeat the attempt.

'Do you know why there are only seven on the team?' said Stelios.
'I don't know anything about football. Isn't that normal?' I replied.
'No, but we couldn't afford twelve T-shirts!' he said.

I spoke to a West Bank colleague the other day and asked about Tristan.
They think now that he will probably live. There isn't really any more
news; he is conscious again, and he has some movement on his right
side, but none on his left, and it's possible he never will. Anarchists
Against the Wall are providing care and support for his family and
girlfriend. Sasha said it helps everyone a lot that Tristan's mum and
dad totally understand and support his work in the West Bank.

When Tom was shot in the head, Jenny said it felt to her like he was
gone from that moment, though physically he lived another year, in
a coma, before his death. Of ISM's injured over the years, we've not
had to face the reality of brain damage leading to serious disability;
the severest long-term injury not leading to death that I am aware of
was Brian Avery, who underwent major facial reconstructive surgery
after being shot in the West Bank city of Jenin. Two of us here in Gaza
now have in the past been shot with live ammunition, and both injuries
were potentially life-threatening at the time, but the long-term effects
have been minimal in comparison.

Tomorrow morning I am on ambulance training shift with our
teacher Anwar – he manages the Rafah station – and most of the
others are farming at Khoza'a. I hope I don't get to practise anything
on anyone there. Someone recently commented that I sound like I am
becoming more edgy about danger, as I get closer to leaving and it
occurs to me I might come out of here alive after all. But actually, while
we try to be practically prepared for our own injury, the edginess all of
us feel is much more for our Palestinian friends, like Sobhe and Yara,
and the farmers for whom we can offer nothing but our presence, as
they work daily in fear.

During the war, I remember saying to someone that my feeling for
Gaza was what you might feel for an orphaned child, bewildered

at finding herself alone, without protection, for no reason she can understand. It will feel terribly wrong to walk away.

On a bright note... Sobhe tells us Mohammed who was shot in the foot has been able to get back out on his motorbike. On a not so bright note, April 12 is the beginning of an international week of solidarity with the approximately 10,000 Palestinian men, women, and children held in Israeli prison, many without charge... I was telling another friend today the story of Yara confiscating the soldier's gun. He told me his aunt had done the same thing during the first Intifada – only her soldier had been an Israeli general, *and* she actually broke the gun. In response, the army arrested her husband and sent him to prison for eight months.

APRIL 13

When we began our first-level medic course here in Khan Younis Red Crescent, we found a lot of unintentional black humour in the training slides, which were developed in America. The smiling medic pairs, wheeling Aryan children – sitting up and looking unaccountably cheerful – into shiny ambulances, seemed like some sort of sick joke.

One of the slides illustrating 'be aware of danger at the scene' showed two police cautiously approaching a bloke who looked perhaps mildly irritated (the same way I feel when approached by the police, actually). A second 'danger at the scene' picture showed a woman paramedic entering a pub to find a man lying on the floor, and the other patrons watching with vague interest from their bar stools. We volunteered captions:

'You don't want to do it like *that*, love,' I offered.

'He's bin there a week now...' drawled Ewa.

No detached limbs in these pictures, no 'second strike' rockets falling on these medics and their patients, no snipers aiming at them. They seemed more in danger of boredom than anything else.

By contrast, we latched on immediately to Khan Younis's single copy of *Save Lives, Save Limbs*, by Dr Mads Gilbert – who spent January working tirelessly here in Gaza – and colleagues. This handbook was developed to teach and support village medics in countries where people are injured every day from leftover mines. (Incidentally, I have read that globally, mines are being laid faster than mine clearance organisations are removing them. Once again, giving money to charities is useless if we don't address injustice and violence politically.)

Actually on one of the first pages of the book they point out how meaningless pictures of pink smiling blood-free patients are to most people in most countries, and proceed to use illustrations of visibly poor, Asian, injured folks and medics, with accurately torn and missing limbs. Considering how grim its topic, this is a warm and inspiring book, taking emergency care out of the hands of distant experts and putting it into the hands of the injured person's comrades and neighbours, emphasising respect and psychological support for all, and alerting locals to be aware of possible hidden agendas of aid arrangements coming from outside.

We have very much enjoyed our course and our teachers, who have found time for us in amongst their long hours and low pay (if any; many medics are volunteers) and Red Crescent job cuts (it hardly seems the time, does it?). Two out of three of our teachers have been in Israeli prison, but then what Palestinian man hasn't? One told us of coming back via Egypt, having gone outside with his wife to get medical treatment for his small son who has cerebral palsy, and being arrested as he entered Gaza, back when the border was more directly controlled by Israel and not ostensibly by Egypt.

He then spent three years in prison, a lot of it sharing a small room with ten people; their sentences from 25 to 99 years. While he was in there, his father died, and his fourth child was born.

'What were you in prison for?' I asked.

'I don't know exactly,' he said. 'I think it was because we picked up a dead fighter in the ambulance, and I locked his gun temporarily in my office because the only other option was to leave it lying where we found him, which would have been irresponsible. Somehow they turned that into the accusation that I was selling weapons.'

Another teacher, when he was a teenager, was doing very well in high school and planned to study medicine in Turkey, but then was picked up for throwing stones at soldiers (in David-and-Goliath tradition, except that stones thrown by lads other than David are usually completely ineffective, since soldiers wear body armour). He was imprisoned as punishment, and banned from leaving Gaza. So he never did become a doctor.

The good news: we did track down some rented crutches for Yara.

APRIL 15

I am spending this week saying a thousand goodbyes. I tried to give people short notice of my last visits, in the hope of avoiding gifts. But you can't stop Palestinians giving you things, because if they didn't (or can't afford to) buy something for you, then they will raid their own belongings for something they think you might like. Last week this included a fancy bra, which I was instructed to quickly hide before the menfolk came back into the room! But most valuable to me are the many dear friends who quietly announced themselves to be my brother or my sister, only waiting the chance to help me with anything I might need in life.

Something I particularly felt proud of was my last tea-drinking with Eva's and my *tai kwon do* teacher. He speaks almost no English, and our mutual friend Saleh (who does) and Eva generally are the conduit between us for easy chatting. Neither of them could make our last meeting, and my teacher and I later admitted to uneasiness about facing an hour of communication by ourselves. But we were proud of how great we did! I *can* talk Arabic now – ok, not fluently, and no doubt my conversation contains a lot of nonsense and some appalling grammar, but I can communicate, and I'm so happy about that.

I don't want to go. But I want to do this midwifery degree, and they won't defer my place a second time. Someone was telling me about an old Arabic word for midwife, which translates as 'the one who brings the soul from the soul'.

APRIL 20

...after two days at the border, I have managed to exit Gaza via Rafah into Egypt.

This is an excerpt from a post I wrote in September 2008:

The outdoor restaurant overlooking the sea has been nicknamed 'Casablanca without the alcohol' by Dr Bill. Here, we internationals and Palestinians alike sit, looking out over the moonlit water, sharing *argeelah* and rumours about the Rafah border. Will it open? If so, when? And for who? People tell each other about what documents they have obtained, what connections they have made, which consulate may be arranging a visa for them. They show pictures of husbands, wives, children, lovers who are waiting in other lands.

Until now, this border with Egypt, the only way Palestinians with no other passport may come or go from Gaza, has opened 8 days this year. But we hear it will again, for two days, before Ramadan begins. Saturday and Sunday. No, Tuesday until Thursday. Definitely Saturday, Sunday is unsure. Saturday, but only for the sick travelling for treatment. No, Saturday for foreign passport holders, Sunday for the sick. Maybe also Monday, the first day of Ramadan. No, not Monday. But only if your name is on the published list. No, you can try even if your name is not published...

I first fought the Rafah border last year, and for a month, the Rafah border – or should I say Egypt – or should I say Israel? – won. Eventually, quite randomly, a Danish consulate rep kindly extracted me from it, along with my Danish colleague. My Cairo Australian consulate folks had made various unsuccessful efforts all that month, never failing however to remind me, 'But you *do* realise our website advises Australian tourists that Gaza is *not* a safe place to visit?' which used to leave me rather nonplussed. Considering the two years' work I'd put into getting here by sea, the reasons I'd come, and the work I was doing, I seemed to have about as little to do with tourism as possible. This year, to my relief, at least my Tel Aviv consulate contacts seemed to be aware of the concept of human rights work, and one was even interested enough to have a look at my blog, bless her.

Writing about this border, I've had to self censor. I need the border on my side again in the future, especially if someone I care about inside Gaza is injured and I want to get to them quickly, something I think about every day. So there'll be no political analysis about the border from me here. But I'll *complain* about it gladly!

You never know when – or for long periods of time, if – there will be a border open on any given day at all. Generally there is about two days' notice. So if you are a Palestinian trying to leave Gaza, you remain in a sort of limbo, having said your proper goodbyes perhaps a long time before you can leave – *if* you can leave. If you are a student with a scholarship awaiting you in the outside world, months might pass, every day with the expectation of leaving loved ones behind for three years... or maybe not.

Palestinians have to apply for exit to the Gaza authorities, with all the necessary documents proving they have permission to go somewhere else, and then hopefully they get allotted a place on a border-destined bus, with an early morning collection. Foreigners however can simply turn up at the first border gate on the Palestinian side under their own steam, and if you are me, with a government liaison person on a phone you can wave at a border guard, you might only wait two hours getting sunburnt. (Last year, heading to my first unsuccessful border attempt, I found myself sped through that gate in a smart car, sirens wailing, due to being with Lauren Booth, Tony Blair's sister-in-law. But I decided that was a bit embarrassing and uncalled for and to be avoided in the future.)

The buses can end up being bed for the night as well, as happened last year, when Adam from Denmark and I joined the thousands of Palestinians who'd passed the Palestinian border and were waiting for the Egypt gate to deign to open so they could at least be considered for entry. Most of the buses this year looked to be heading for the same scenario, when I – on bus number 4 out of 36 – passed through the Egypt gate at 4pm, after a six-hour wait while the Egyptians apparently processed all of three preceding buses.

Last year, the Palestinian border guys attempted to arrange for me to sleep in a border compound room, but when I realised they would be ousting about twelve male staff on my behalf, I refused and stomped off back to my bus seat. When they found me about half an hour later, and told me in horrified tones that I couldn't sleep there, I lost my temper (something I often do with authorities generally and which the ones here endure with remarkable patience) and pulled out my honorary Palestinian passport.

'If all the other Palestinians can, then so can I!' I said.

After a moment's thought, they either decided I had a point, or was too much of a pain to persist with, and left me be.

I am quite bendy, and have much practice sleeping in a tangled knot on a bus. But sick people were on these buses, hoping to head outside for treatment. Elderly people were here too. I remember watching the patient dignity with which grandparents, knowing there was no chance of sleep despite an exhausting day of waiting in the heat and with another ahead, sat bolt upright in their narrow seats, cradling the smallest children, so that at least they could sleep in comfort.

Palestinian kids. I don't know what it is about them, maybe it's growing up being one of about ten usually, so whinging isn't likely to get you anything other than a thump on the head from your next-oldest sibling. But they seem to have learned not to ask for much, to resign themselves patiently to conditions that kids from the UK wouldn't put up with for five minutes. Ten, twenty hours on a stationary bus? No toys? Little food or water? Quietness, is what you get from Palestinian kids. I don't know, maybe they just think to their small selves, 'No one's dying. No-one's dropping rockets on me. I'm on the credit side here.'

This time, the Egyptians handed out bottles of water – that didn't happen last year in the summer. Remembering that, I'd brought my own and, prior to the handout, had passed it round the back of the bus, resulting in about five bottles being forced on me when our bus was later given its ration.

Sometimes the bus engine would actually start, and the few folks that had risked going outside for a breather would leap back in with alacrity. But generally it wouldn't mean anything, or it would mean a metre's progress and then off would go the engine again.

There seemed to be a complicated system whereby Egyptian guards required everyone to have a seat, and there to be no bags in aisles, despite there being more bags than bag space and more people than seats. This made for a sort of energetic shuffling of people and bags anytime the Egyptians paid us any attention – some clearly enjoying that their demands we were so desperate to fulfil were in fact impossible, and some sympathising, and suggesting compromises, or accepting men sitting on bags in aisles as meeting the requirements.

Getting through the gate, into the Egypt hall, felt like a miracle in itself. Many of the other buses never got that far. You can buy crisps in the Egypt hall. And since you might be spending another six hours there – or be turned around and sent back again – then you're pretty grateful for crisps.

This year, Jackie, an American visitor, and I exited into Egypt at the end of our second day of trying. Egyptian security had found the co-ordination papers for me they didn't find the first day. Ewa was refused entry a second time, so Caoimhe decided not to take up her own permission to leave, planning to return with Ewa to face an exhausting third day of doing it all again, supposing the relevant documents had arrived – or been found – by then. And supposing day three of border opening didn't get cancelled. No-one negotiates better than Caoimhe – you swiftly learn that if she mutters 'don't say *anything*' out of the side of her mouth at you, it's the absolute best thing you can do for yourself – and even she couldn't extract Ewa.

Turning back with them, on the buses of the refused, were students who had all their documents totally sorted and confirmed. Patients whose operations are awaiting them. One young man on crutches, with two explosive bullet wounds in his leg since the war. His surgeon, a British doctor, wasn't allowed in and he wasn't allowed out to see her. This seemed to have something to do with him having a beard. Bearded men the world over can tell you this is not synonymous with being a Hamas combatant. It's like of those 'false logic' problems they give you in high school maths. 'All Hamas militants wear beards. Therefore, all bearded men are Hamas militants.' Nuh-uh. At least he can try shaving off his beard. But what can the students and patients, with all their papers present and correct, try next month? If there is an open day next month.

As we left, a woman that Jackie had been chatting to in the hours of waiting in the Egyptian hall, shepherded her kids through the exit to Egypt, and Jackie turned to congratulate her, but the woman was weeping. They were allowed, but not her husband.

'*Marra tanya* – next time?' we asked. The woman shook her head hopelessly.

I hate borders. I hate walls, I hate boundaries. I hate anything that prevents the free movement of people *wherever* they want to go. I hate that we must clutch our passports tight everywhere we walk in this world, knowing that a person without the 'right' documents is apparently no longer a person at all. I hate anything that keeps us separate from our hopes, our dreams, and those we love.

There is an Arabic word, *badri*, that literally means 'early', but people say it to guests. As in, what's this? You've been enjoying our hospitality for only eight hours and already you're *leaving*? *Badri!*

On my last day in Gaza City, when I left my apartment and emerged onto the street to gaze at the sea for one last time, an elderly man passed me. With one glance he took in my foreignness, my backpack, and the fact that it was Rafah opening day. He looked back over his shoulder, and smilingly shook his head in reprimand.

'*Badri*,' he said.

AFTERWORD

Richard Falk

United Nations Special Rapporteur for the Human Rights Council
in the Occupied Palestinian Territories

Sharyn Lock provides her readers with a moving and understated account of her real time experience of Gaza and Gazans living and dying under Israeli occupation. The narrative is highlighted by the 22 days of sustained attack by the Israeli military forces (December 27, 2008–January 18, 2009) that adds an indispensable dimension of understanding to our awareness of that terrible ordeal. By witnessing, participating, and sharing in the vulnerability of the 1.5 million Palestinians trapped in the impoverished and crowded killing fields of the Gaza Strip Sharyn Lock manages to humanize the inhuman. In doing so she creates an unforgettable profile of the fear mingled with love that existed among Gazans constantly living in gruesome conditions that have not yet been mitigated to this day despite the myriad of calls from political leaders and moral authority figures around the world.

How the Israeli psyche can stand its role as cruel perpetrator of such an orgy of suffering inflicted on an entrapped civilian population of whom more than half are children has become a grotesque mystery for me. A juridical searchlight has been shined on the Gaza attacks of last winter by the release of the Goldstone Report on September 15, 2009. This report with its methodical examination of the grounds for war crimes allegations leveled at Israel, but also at Hamas, is a model of careful, balanced inquiry conducted by respected experts eager to convey and act upon the truth; nothing more, but also nothing less. Its 575 pages of factual presentation and legal analysis are a much less readable account of the same events than are Sharyn Lock's daily journal entries and edited blogs. Both report on an orgy of one-sided violence directed at an essentially defenseless society, and essentially confirm one another.

The fury of Israel's official repudiation of the Goldstone Report exhibits the extent to which a raw nerve was touched, perhaps illustrating the old adage that 'the truth hurts.' For the Israeli leadership, including the Prime Minister and Minister of Defense, to claim that the report is 'a gift to terrorism' or a challenge to Israel's right to defend itself repudiates the very notion that there are legal and moral limits to the way war is waged in the twenty-first century. For what the Goldstone Report contends, and what the testimony of IDF soldiers reinforces in the powerful pamphlet, 'Breaking the Silence,' is that Israeli rules of engagement and operational tactics on the Gaza battlefield deliberately targeted unarmed civilians and used hyper-modern weaponry in areas where civilians were known to be with the intention of destroying much of the already strained civilian infrastructure of Gaza, including its electricity generators, educational institutions, medical facilities, UN buildings, mosques. Sharyn Lock puts the truth of the situation in a single devastating sentence that is undoubtedly too simple for the legal mind:

'Everything I have seen suggests that the Israeli army doesn't even understand the concept of "innocent civilians"' (p. 64).

Such destruction abetted a situation of extreme deprivation that has persisted at least since mid-2007 when a comprehensive blockade was imposed that has allowed only sub-subsistence levels of food, medicine, and fuel to enter Gaza. Without the several hundred tunnels into Egypt, as well as the vital food and services provided by the UNRWA (UN Relief and Works Agency) presence, the ordeal in the Gaza Strip would have long ago eventuated in a genocidal catastrophe. This blockade has even been used to disallow donated aid to bring such basic building materials as cement, glass, and bricks into Gaza to repair some of the damage done by the attacks of last winter, which amounts to a new kind of post-conflict crime, that of disallowing civilian recovery from military devastation.

The Goldstone Report, essentially a fact-finding mission, that does recommend implementing accountability for the commission of war crimes in Gaza challenges the UN to live up finally to its own Charter, to end the regime of impunity for politically powerful leaders of sovereign states. It recommends making use of the International Criminal Court to the extent necessary, and also proposes prosecution of alleged war criminals in national courts should serious suspects enter national territory. This latter recommendation, known as 'universal jurisdiction,' was prominently invoked back in 1998 when Spain requested that Britain detain and extradite the former Chilean dictator, Augusto Pinochet, to face criminal charges in Madrid. In 1962 Israel itself relied on universal jurisdiction when it prosecuted and executed Adolph Eichmann for Nazi crimes committed in Germany before the state of Israel came into existence. Surely, if the UN is to supplant the regime of force by the rule of law, it should fully implement the Goldstone recommendations.

At the time of writing (November 2009), the future of the Goldstone Report is uncertain. The UN General Assembly is likely to endorse its recommendations, but then what? It is clear that the United States will continue brazenly to use its geopolitical muscle to ensure Israeli impunity, standing irresponsibly ready to wield the veto in the Security Council if any effort is made to *enforce* Goldstone. My own skeptical view is that the UN will fail the Goldstone test, and that its call for accountability will not be heeded, and the peoples of the world will be again reminded that international criminal law is only meant for the weak and defeated. In this respect, the inter-governmental system although fashioning the international legal order remains the domain of unchecked power and violence. Within the UN this means that geopolitics trumps law and justice, while the bodies pile up.

It should be realized that the Goldstone Report leans over backwards to overlook the multiple criminality of Israel's occupation policies associated with the attacks on Gaza of 2008–09. For instance, despite the existence of an effective ceasefire, along with a Hamas offer to extend it for up to ten years, Israel's dubious claim of necessary self-defense was uncritically accepted by the Goldstone Report, and inquiry was limited to determining whether the use of force was excessive and directed at unlawful targets. As a result, the core international law question was never raised – was this justifiable use of defensive force or was it aggression, a crime against the peace since the Nuremberg Judgment in 1945. Furthermore, the Goldstone Report never criminalizes the Israeli failure to allow Gazan civilians to leave the war zone, and become refugees. To deny civilians a refugee option is rare in the annals of modern warfare. It meant that every civilian in Gaza whether or not wounded experienced the severe trauma of being exposed day and night to the terror of these essentially unopposed and relentless Israeli attacks from land, sea, and air.

International law does not clearly address this Gaza reality in which one-sided violence is undertaken by Israel without any serious military resistance. The casualty ratios were over 100:1, and much greater if the wounded are included, and almost encompassing the whole of the Gazan population if mental harm is counted. The conflict was so one-sided that it hardly counts as a war, where normally reciprocity between actors lends weight to prescriptions for mutual restraints on tactics and weapons. When one side is all powerful, choosing how and what to destroy at its discretion without any serious worry about retaliation, the relationship resembles *torture* not *war*. The international law of war because it is shaped to such an extent by the victors and the strong has been slow to impose restraints on the violence of the powerful. It is shocking, yet revealing, that even nuclear weapons, despite being massively indiscriminate in their destructiveness, have neither been prohibited nor renounced. Virtually every page of Sharyn Lock's testimony transmits the tearful reality of this utter Palestinian vulnerability.

What gives a radiance to this deeply felt autobiographical account of Sharyn Lock's Gaza experience is the tacit comparison between the sterility of inter-governmental responsiveness and the creative engagement of civil society with Palestinian suffering. Her participation in the International Solidarity Movement, whose members have died or been maimed in their roles as nonviolent volunteers, is notable for its transnational bonds of love, as well as for its affirmation of the human spirit. Her involvement with the Free Gaza Movement demonstrates that civil society activists, including from Israel, who gather the resources to send boats with medical supplies to Gaza, were prepared to break the unlawful blockade of Gaza in a manner that governments are afraid or unable to do.

What is conveyed indirectly is the tragedy and the truth of the Palestinian ordeal: the only hope that presently exists for this long beleaguered people arises from the commitment and work of people like Sharyn Lock and her collaborators all over the world. The UN shows neither the capacity nor the political will to implement its own resolutions, encouraging the false belief that only violent resistance can end the Israeli occupation and produce peace. Governments are subject to the geopolitical discipline imposed by military power: so far only Libya has attempted to send humanitarian relief to Gaza, and turned away as soon as its cargo ship with supplies was refused entry by Israel, not willing to risk a confrontation.

Sharyn Lock's real achievement is to convey the wisdom of the great Jewish thinker Abraham Heschel: 'Few are guilty, but all are responsible.' The fate of the Palestinian people continues, of course, to depend mainly on their own efforts. But these efforts are being increasingly supported by the Palestinian success in the second war, The Legitimacy War being fought on a global battlefield. It is the authentic successor to the anti-apartheid campaign that eventually contributed to realizing the impossible, nonviolently dismantling the racist regime in South Africa. The growing strength of BDS (boycott, divestment, and sanctions) initiatives around the world is expressive of this legitimacy dimension in the Palestinian struggle. The Goldstone Report is a major victory for the Palestinians in The Legitimacy War that should have shown the Israelis by now that military dominance and political oppression bring their country neither security nor peace. To reach a just and sustainable solution is far from automatic. It will depend, as Heschel's imperative instructs us, on people of conscience throughout the world becoming warriors in The Legitimacy War. There are many opportunities: not attending cultural or academic events with Israeli performers, refusing touristic visits to Israel, boycotting products and companies that do business in Israel, and lobbying their governments to withhold weapons and impose sanctions so long as Israel defies international law and morality. For the clarity of this teaching about nonviolent struggle and engagement I will long remain grateful to Sharyn Lock!

Santa Barbara, California
November 2009

NOTES

INTRODUCTION

1. http://www.palsolidarity.org, viewed August 2009.
2. ATG 2005/8, 'Palestine & The Palestinians'.
3. Bassam Abu-Sharif and Uzi Mahnaimi, *Tried By Fire*, Little, Brown, 1995.
4. Khaled Hroub, *Hamas: A Beginner's Guide*, Pluto Press, 2006.
5. Ibid.
6. Defence For Children International press release, June 8, 2006.
7. Red Cross, quoted in the *Independent*, November 15, 2008.
8. CARE International press release, March 6, 2008.
9. WHO press release, 'Norway provides medical supplies to WHO response to Gaza crisis', January 4, 2009.
10. BBC News, 'Sewage flood causes Gaza deaths', March 27, 2007.
11. http://www.globalsecurity.org/military/world/para/hamas-qassam.htm

CHAPTER 1

1. *Ha'aretz*, 'Israel fears European ship may sail to Gaza to "break siege"', July 28, 2008.
2. Ramattan is a Palestinian news agency with an office in Gaza.
3. http://fishingunderfire.blogspot.com/search/label/boat%20ramed.
4. President of the UN at UN General Assembly, http://un.org/ga/president/63/statements/idn21008.shtml.

CHAPTER 2

1. http://www.arabnews.com/?page=4&section=0&article=117065&d=8&m=12&y=2008.
2. Karen Abu Zayd, Commissioner General of UNRWA.

3. http://www.unhchr.ch/huricane/huricane.nsf/0/183ED1610B2BCB80C12575 1A002B06B2?opendocument.
4. The term 'martyr' is used routinely in Palestine to describe anyone killed as a result of the Israeli occupation. It does not only refer to fighters or suicide bombers, as is sometimes implied in the Western press.
5. Al Jazeera English, 'Livni hints at Gaza military action', December 25, 2008.

CHAPTER 3

1. Many differing figures exist for the casualties resulting from the first waves of the Israeli attack, but numbers given here are similar to those quoted by the *Jerusalem Post*: '230 dead in first day of Gaza offensive', December 27, 2008.
2. http://www.ynetnews.com/articles/0,7340,L-3647005,00.html.
3. The official name for the Israeli army is the IDF – Israeli Defence Forces. However, they are routinely referred to by pro-Palestine activists as the IOF – Israeli Occupation Forces.

CHAPTER 5

1. Amnesty International, 'Operation Cast Lead: 22 days of death and destruction', July 2009.
2. Al Jazeera English, 'Israeli jets bomb Gaza targets', February 2, 2009.

CHAPTER 6

1. Binyamin Netanyahu was elected for a second time as Israeli PM in February 2009.
2. *Ha'aretz*, 'IDF confirms army dog bit Palestinian during West Bank raid', February 22, 2009.
3. *Guardian*, 'Israel accused of war crimes over 12-hour assault on Gaza village', January 18, 2009.
4. See January 22.
5. See January 8–10.

6. See January 27.
7. Rachel Corrie, a US citizen aged 23, was killed when she was crushed by a Caterpillar D9 bulldozer which she was trying to prevent from demolishing a Palestinian home.
8. 'For Rachel, 6 years later' – Joe Carr.

CHAPTER 7

1. *Ha'aretz*, 'IDF soldiers ordered to shoot at Gaza rescuers, note says', March 22, 2009.
2. See December 30/31.
3. Little Sara was born to our Jabalia friends in October 2009.

FURTHER INFORMATION

http://palsolidarity.org/
http://freegaza.org/
http://electronicintifada.net/
http://fishingunderfire.blogspot.com/
http://farmingunderfire.blogspot.com/
http://stopthewall.org/
http://sumoud.tao.ca/
http://defendtherescuers.wordpress.com/
http://awalls.org/
http://btselem.org/English/
http://ingaza.wordpress.com/
http://talestotell.wordpress.com/
http://closedzone.com/
http://ctrlaltshift.co.uk/video/no-way-through-documentary

INDEX

Compiled by Sue Carlton